Recipes for

Ground Beef

and other ground meats

By the Editors of Sunset Books and Sunset Magazine

Lane Books • Menlo Park, California

Edited by Judith A. Gaulke

Special Consultant
Joan Griffiths, Staff Home Economist, Sunset Magazine

Design: John Flack
Illustrations: Marsha Kline
Cover Photograph: Milton Halberstadt

Home Economics Editor, Sunset Magazine: Annabel Post

Executive Editor, Sunset Books: David E. Clark

Second Printing January 1974
Copyright © Lane Magazine & Book Company, Menlo Park, California
Second Edition 1973. World rights reserved.

Contents

A Hamburger for all Reasons

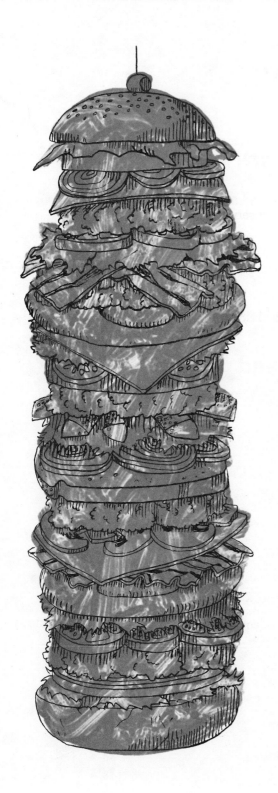

Tarragon Beef Burgers

You bake these patties, then serve them topped with thin slices of avocado.

1½ pounds lean ground beef
 1 teaspoon salt
 ¼ pepper
 3 tablespoons instant toasted onion
 3 tablespoons tarragon wine vinegar
 6 slices Swiss or Cheddar cheese
 6 hamburger buns, split, buttered, and toasted
 1 medium-sized avocado, peeled and
    thinly sliced

Mix together the beef, salt, and pepper. Shape into 6 patties and place in a shallow baking pan. Sprinkle meat with onions and vinegar. Bake, uncovered, in a 375° oven 12 to 15 minutes for rare, 20 minutes for medium, or 25 minutes for well done. Arrange cheese on the top half of each bun and place in the oven to melt during the last few minutes the patties are cooking. Place a patty on the other half of the bun and top with slices of avocado. Makes 6 servings.

Blue Cheeseburger

Chill the cheese-seasoned meat mixture for several hours to allow the flavors to blend; then shape into patties and broil.

 ¼ pound blue cheese
 3 pounds lean ground beef
 ½ cup minced chives or green onions, including
    part of the tops
 ¼ teaspoon liquid hot pepper seasoning
 1 teaspoon Worcestershire
 1 teaspoon coarse ground pepper
1½ teaspoons salt
 1 teaspoon dry mustard
12 French rolls or hamburger buns, buttered
    and toasted

Crumble cheese into meat. Add chives, hot pepper seasoning, Worcestershire, pepper, salt, and mustard; mix together lightly. Cover and chill 2 hours to give flavors time to blend, then lightly shape the meat into 12 patties. Broil or barbecue about 4 inches from heat or hot glowing coals until browned on both sides or done to your liking 4 or 5 minutes on each side for medium-rare. Serve on toasted buttered French rolls or buns. Makes 12 servings.

Giant Barbecued Hamburger

This dramatic sandwich will serve 8 people. Its base can be the inner slice of a whole round loaf of French bread or a large sesame-covered peda loaf cut horizontally. A 2½-pound grilled ground beef patty sits on top. To serve, cut into pie-shaped wedges and eat with a knife and fork.

1 round flat loaf (1 lb. 6 oz. size) sourdough
    French bread (about 10 inches in diameter)
    or 1 round peda loaf
  Butter
2½ pounds lean ground beef
  1 teaspoon each garlic salt and onion salt
  3 tablespoons each mayonnaise and
    chile sauce
  1 cup shredded iceberg lettuce
  1 sweet red onion
  2 large tomatoes
  1 avocado
  8 pitted jumbo-sized ripe olives
  ½ cup shredded sharp Cheddar cheese

Slice the top and bottom crusts from the loaf of French bread, leaving a center slice about ¾ inch thick for the base of the hamburger. (You can use the two outer crusts for accompanying bread or save for other uses.) Or cut peda bread horizontally making the bottom crust at least ¾ inch thick. Butter the bread slice or peda bread halves.

Mix the ground beef with garlic salt and onion salt and shape into a patty 1 inch larger than the diameter of the bread base to allow for shrinkage when meat cooks. Place meat patty in a large hinged grill. Place on a barbecue grill about 4 inches above moderately-hot coals and cook until underside is browned (about 6 minutes). Turn and cook other side. (If you don't have a wire grill, use two spatulas to slide the patty onto a baking sheet. Place a second baking sheet on top

and turn baking sheets over so the cooked side of meat is up. Then slide meat patty back onto the grill to cook the other side.)

Cook meat on barbecue until the inside is done to your liking when slashed (about 6 minutes longer for medium-rare). Meanwhile, heat and toast buttered bread slice or peda halves on grill. Place toasted bread or bottom of peda loaf on a wooden board or platter.

Spread bread with mayonnaise and chile sauce, then cover with lettuce and top with barbecued meat. Peel and thinly slice onion and arrange rings on the meat. Peel and slice tomato thinly and lay on top. Peel and slice avocado and arrange in a pinwheel design from the center. Garnish with olives and sprinkle with cheese. Serve French bread sandwich open-faced or cover peda bread bottom with its top. To serve, cut in wedges. Makes 8 servings.

Western Chile Cheeseburger

Our cover photo shows off this mouth-watering hamburger crowned with melted cheese.

1½ pounds lean ground beef
  ⅓ cup each finely chopped onion and fine dry
    bread crumbs
  2 tablespoons seeded and finely chopped canned
    California green chiles
  1 egg
  ¾ teaspoon salt
  ¼ teaspoon pepper
  ½ teaspoon each ground cumin seed and
    oregano leaves
  4 slices Swiss or jack cheese, each about
    3 inches square
  4 slices French bread, lightly buttered
  4 crisp lettuce leaves
  4 to 8 large tomato slices, cut ¼ inch thick
  4 sweet gherkin pickles

Combine the ground beef, onion, crumbs, chiles, egg, salt, pepper, cumin, and oregano. Divide into 4 equal-sized portions; shape each into a thick patty about 4 inches in diameter.

Place on a grill about 4 inches above a bed of medium-hot glowing coals. Cook 4 to 5 minutes, turn, place a slice of cheese on top, and cook 4 to 5 minutes more for medium-rare or until done to your liking. Toast bread slices, buttered side down, on the grill during the last few minutes.

To serve, place a toasted bread slice on each plate, top each with a lettuce leaf, 1 or 2 tomato slices, and a cheese-topped patty. Garnish with a gherkin. Serve open-faced to eat with a knife and fork. Makes 4 servings.

Oriental Hamburgers

You marinate these beef patties in a soy-seasoned sauce for an hour or so before broiling.

½ cup each soy sauce and water
1 clove garlic, minced or mashed
2 teaspoons grated fresh ginger
2 tablespoons Worcestershire
6 tablespoons firmly packed brown sugar
3 pounds lean ground beef
8 rectangular French rolls
  Thinly sliced tomatoes
  Green pepper rings

Combine soy sauce, water, garlic, ginger, Worcestershire, and brown sugar. Shape ground beef into 8 log-shaped meat patties (to fit the long French rolls). Pour soy mixture over the meat and marinate for 1 to 1½ hours. Lift patties from marinade, drain briefly, and grill about 4 inches above hot coals, or broil 4 inches from heat, 4 to 5 minutes on each side for medium-rare or until done to your liking. Baste several times with the marinade. Split rolls and toast them on the grill or under the broiler. Fill rolls with the meat patties, sliced tomatoes, and green pepper rings. Makes 8 servings.

Barbecued Cheddar Burgers

The cheese hides between two thin patties in this cheeseburger.

2 pounds lean ground beef
2 tablespoons instant minced onion
2 teaspoons each Worcestershire and
  prepared mustard
1 teaspoon salt
½ teaspoon pepper
1½ cups shredded sharp Cheddar cheese
  Melted butter
6 hamburger buns, split, buttered, and toasted

Thoroughly mix together the ground beef, onion, Worcestershire, mustard, salt, and pepper. Shape into 12 thin patties. Put ¼ cup of the shredded cheese in a mound on top of each of 6 patties; top with another meat patty and press edges together to seal. Grill about 4 inches above a bed of hot coals 4 to 5 minutes on each side for medium-rare or until done to your liking. Baste with melted butter; turn only once. Serve on toasted buns. Makes 6 servings.

Beef and Cheese Buns

You assemble these hearty sandwiches ahead, ready to heat and serve.

1 pound lean ground beef
1 tablespoon chopped green onion
¾ teaspoon salt
¼ teaspoon pepper
2 tablespoons catsup
  Cheese Topping (recipe follows)
4 round hamburger buns, split and
  lightly buttered

Combine the ground beef, onion, salt, pepper, and catsup; mix well and shape into 4 patties. Place on the rack of a broiler pan; broil about 4 inches from heat until browned on both sides and done to your liking (4 to 5 minutes total for rare). Let cool while you prepare the cheese topping.

Place each meat patty on a bun half; top with about ¼ of the cheese topping and remaining bun half. Wrap each bun tightly in foil; refrigerate as long as overnight.

To heat, place wrapped buns in a 350° oven for about 30 minutes or until meat is heated through. Makes 4 servings.

Cheese Topping. Combine 1 cup shredded sharp Cheddar cheese, 2 tablespoons soft butter, 1½ teaspoons catsup, ½ teaspoon prepared mustard, and 1 tablespoon finely chopped green onion.

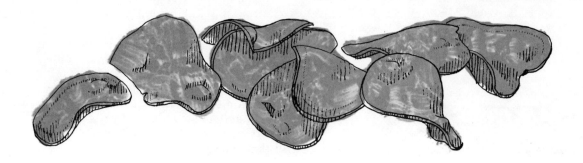

Man-Sized Burgers

Chile con carne, shredded cheese, and chile sauce are enclosed between two patties for this meaty burger. The filled patties are broiled, then topped with onion rings, more cheese, and chile sauce, and put back under the broiler for final browning.

> 2 pounds lean ground beef
> ½ teaspoon salt
> ¼ teaspoon pepper
> 1 teaspoon Worcestershire
> 1 can (about 1 lb.) chile con carne with beans
> 1½ cups shredded Cheddar cheese
> ⅓ cup chile sauce
> 6 thin slices onion, each dipped in salad oil

Combine the ground beef with salt, pepper, and Worcestershire; shape into 12 patties, each about ¼ inch thick. In a pan, heat chile con carne. Also have ready the Cheddar cheese, chile sauce, and onion slices. On each of six patties, spoon 1½ tablespoons of the chile con carne, 2 tablespoons of the cheese, and 1 teaspoon of the chile sauce. Top each with another patty, pressing the edges to seal. Broil about 4 inches from heat for 4 to 5 minutes on each side for medium-rare or until done to your liking.

Remove from broiler and top each with an oiled onion slice, sprinkle with remaining cheese, and top with remaining chile sauce. Put back under broiler about 2 minutes or until top is bubbly. Reheat remaining chile con carne to serve with the meat. Makes 6 servings.

Polynesian Hamburgers

Broiled beef patties on English muffins are topped with tropical fruits for this colorful supper sandwich.

> 1½ pounds lean ground beef
>   Salt
> 6 tablespoons bottled barbecue sauce
> 6 English muffins, split
>   About ½ cup (¼ lb.) melted butter or margarine
> 2 bananas
> 1 can (about 14 oz.) pineapple chunks, drained
> 1 small green pepper

Shape meat into 6 patties, slightly larger than the muffins. Sprinkle with salt and place on a broiler rack. Brush with 2 tablespoons of the barbecue sauce. Broil about 4 inches from heat in a preheated broiler for 4 to 5 minutes, turn, brush with 2 more tablespoons sauce, and broil 4 to 5 minutes longer for medium-rare meat or until done to your liking. Brush muffins generously with some of the butter and broil until lightly browned. Transfer meat patties to the muffin bases; set aside the tops.

Slice bananas diagonally, dip in melted butter, and arrange several pieces on top of each meat patty. Dip pineapple chunks in the remaining 2 tablespoons barbecue sauce and spoon over the bananas. Remove seeds and cut pepper into rings, dip in melted butter, and set on top. Place under the broiler about 4 inches below heat just until fruits are hot through and start to brown on the edges. Serve open-faced with muffin tops alongside. Makes 6 servings.

Canadian Bacon Burger

A pungent wine vinegar sauce is spooned over these open-faced sandwiches just before serving.

> ½ cup finely chopped onions
> 3 tablespoons butter or margarine
> 2 pounds lean ground beef
> ¼ cup shredded Parmesan cheese
> 2 tablespoons finely chopped parsley
> ½ teaspoon salt
> 2 egg yolks
> 2 cloves garlic, minced
> 3 ounces Canadian bacon, finely chopped
> 6 slices French bread, toasted
> 2 tablespoons red wine vinegar
> ½ cup dry red wine or regular strength beef broth
>   Chopped green onions
>   Sweet red cherry peppers

In a large frying pan over medium-high heat, sauté the onions in 1 tablespoon of the butter until golden. Transfer onions to a bowl and add the beef, cheese, parsley, salt, egg yolks, garlic, and bacon. Mix together lightly and shape into 6 patties about ¾ inch thick.

(Continued on next page)

Using the same pan, cook hamburgers over medium heat until browned on both sides and done to your liking, about 4 to 5 minutes on each side for medium-rare. Transfer each patty to a slice of toasted French bread and keep warm. Add vinegar to pan and scrape up drippings. Add wine or beef broth and the remaining 2 tablespoons butter. Boil, uncovered, until reduced slightly. Spoon sauce over meat. Garnish each hamburger with a spoonful of chopped green onions and a sweet red cherry pepper. Makes 6 servings.

Whole-Meal Pocket Sandwich

The bread for these sandwiches is called by various names: Arab, Arabic, Armenian, or pocket bread. You can find the bread (fresh or frozen) in many supermarkets in major metropolitan areas of the West or in delicatessens catering to Middle Eastern clientele. Each round of bread makes 2 sandwiches. Allow 1 to 1½ bread rounds for each person.

  1 *pound lean ground lamb*
  1 *teaspoon ground cumin seed*
 ½ *cup chopped onion*
 ½ *teaspoon salt*
  1 *egg*
  2 *tablespoons fine dry bread crumbs*
  1 *tablespoon salad oil*
  4 *rounds pocket (Arab) bread*
    About ½ head romaine
  2 *or 3 tomatoes, cut in wedges*
  1 *thinly sliced mild onion*
  1 *thinly sliced cucumber*
  1 *cup unflavored yogurt*

Mix together in a bowl the lamb, cumin, chopped onion, salt, egg, and bread crumbs. Shape into balls using 1½ tablespoons for each, then flatten balls into ½-inch-thick patties.

Heat oil in a frying pan over medium heat; add patties without crowding, and brown well on both sides. Remove from pan and keep warm; repeat until all are cooked.

To serve, cut bread in half crosswise. Fill each half with meat patties, the tender inner leaves from romaine, tomato wedges, onion slices, and cucumber. Pass yogurt to spoon into each sandwich. Makes 8 sandwiches.

Burgundy-Glazed Hamburgers

Wine sauce redolent of garlic and shallots tops this sautéed hamburger served on an English muffin.

   2 *English muffins*
    Soft butter
1¼ *pounds lean ground beef*
   1 *teaspoon salad oil or olive oil*
   2 *tablespoons chopped shallots or green onions*
   1 *clove garlic, minced*
   1 *teaspoon beef stock base*
  ½ *teaspoon Dijon mustard*
  ¾ *cup dry red wine*
   3 *tablespoons butter*

Split muffins and spread with soft butter. Broil until lightly browned and keep warm on a serving platter.

Shape meat into 4 patties slightly wider than the muffins. Using a large frying pan, cook patties in oil over medium heat, until browned on both sides and done to your liking, about 4 to 5 minutes on each side for medium-rare. (Lower heat and cook longer for medium to well done.) Transfer patties to toasted muffins and keep warm.

Add shallots and garlic to pan; cook a few minutes, stirring. Combine beef stock base, mustard, and wine and pour into pan; boil rapidly, uncovered, until reduced by half. Add the 3 tablespoons butter and heat, stirring, until melted.

Spoon sauce over hamburgers and serve open-faced. Makes 4 servings.

Burgundy-Glazed Hamburgers, French-Style

Omit the English muffins in the preceding recipe. Prepare and cook the patties and sauce as directed. Serve, topped with 1 package (8 oz.) frozen French fried onion rings heated according to package directions.

Pork Sausage Muffin Sandwiches

These sausage patties, served on English muffins, go together quickly for breakfast, lunch, or a light supper.

1½ pounds bulk pork sausage
  6 English muffins
    Butter
  1 large tomato, peeled, and cut into 6 slices
    Grated Parmesan cheese

Divide sausage into 6 equal portions and shape each into a ½-inch-thick patty. Place patties on a broiler pan or a rack in a baking pan. Bake in a 425° oven for 30 minutes.

Split the muffins and place cut side up on a baking sheet; spread with butter, and broil until lightly browned.

To serve, place sausage patties on 6 of the muffin halves, top each with a tomato slice and sprinkle with about 2 teaspoons grated cheese; accompany with remaining muffin halves. Makes 6 servings.

Mushroom Swiss Cheeseburger

Shredded Swiss cheese melts into this beef and mushroom mixture baked on French buns.

  4 French rolls (3 by 5 inches)
    Soft butter
  3 tablespoons butter or margarine
  2 green onions, finely chopped
  ¼ pound mushrooms, sliced
  1 pound lean ground beef
  ½ teaspoon garlic salt
1½ cups (6 oz.) shredded Swiss cheese
    Salt and pepper

Cut rolls in half lengthwise; spread cut surfaces with soft butter. Broil until lightly browned. Melt the 3 tablespoons butter in a frying pan over medium heat. Add onions and mushrooms and sauté just until butter-coated. Remove from heat and let cool. Then mix in ground beef, garlic salt, and cheese. Pat meat mixture evenly on roll bases, covering completely.

Set aside tops of rolls. Bake meat-covered buns in a 450° oven for 20 minutes, or until well browned. Reheat bun tops the last 5 minutes. Season with salt and pepper to taste. Makes 4 servings.

Chile Beef on Cornbread

These chile-flavored ground beef patties are served on sliced cornbread and topped with melted jack cheese, chiles, and tomatoes. Make your own cornbread recipe or use a packaged mix.

  1 pound lean ground beef
  1 teaspoon chile powder
  ½ teaspoon salt
  1 large onion, thinly sliced
  3 tablespoons butter or margarine
  3 thick slices freshly baked cornbread, each cut
     about 2 by 5 inches
    About ¼ pound jack cheese, sliced
  1 canned California green chile, seeded and cut
     in strips
    Cherry tomatoes, cut in halves or sliced
    Bottled taco sauce

Mix beef thoroughly with chile powder and salt and shape into 3 patties, each about 5 inches long and 2 inches wide. Broil about 4 inches from heat for 4 to 5 minutes on each side for medium-rare or until done to your liking. In the meantime, cook the onion in butter over medium heat until soft and lightly browned.

To assemble the sandwiches, spoon onion and butter evenly over slices of cornbread, top each with a beef patty. Cover patty with cheese and broil about 4 inches below heat until cheese melts. Garnish with green chile strips and cherry tomatoes and serve. Pass the taco sauce to pour over each sandwich, if desired. Makes 3 servings.

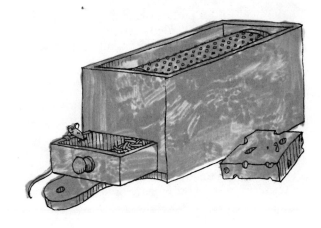

Broiled Beef Patties with Quick Stroganoff Sauce

Mushroom gravy mix is the seasoning short cut to the sour cream sauce you spoon over these broiled patties.

1 pound lean ground beef
1 teaspoon salt
¼ teaspoon pepper
1 package (¾ oz.) mushroom gravy mix
1 tablespoon instant toasted onion
½ teaspoon paprika
½ cup sour cream
3 English muffins, split, buttered, and toasted

Combine ground beef, salt, and pepper, and form into 6 patties. Prepare mushroom gravy according to directions on the package; add toasted onion and paprika. Keep gravy hot (do not boil).

Broil the beef patties, about 4 inches from heat, 4 to 5 minutes on each side for medium-rare or until done to your liking. Just before serving, blend sour cream into mushroom gravy. To serve, place a beef patty on each toasted English muffin half, and spoon sauce over. Makes 6 servings.

Cheeseburger Turnovers

Refrigerator biscuits form the buns for these cheeseburger turnovers.

¾ pound lean ground beef
  Salt and pepper
1 package (8 oz.) refrigerator biscuits
2½ slices (2½ oz.) American cheese
3 tablespoons sweet pickle relish
1 small onion, thinly sliced (optional)
  Mustard (optional)

Shape beef into 5 patties, each about 4 inches in diameter. Sauté over medium heat until browned on both sides. Season with salt and pepper. Remove from heat.

On a lightly floured board, roll each biscuit into a 5-inch round. Place each patty on a biscuit, and cover with ½ slice of cheese. Spread with 1½ teaspoons relish; add slices of onion, if desired. Cover with one of the remaining biscuits; moisten edges with water and pinch to seal. Prick top of biscuits two or three times. Place on an ungreased baking sheet and bake, uncovered, in a 375° oven for 15 to 18 minutes or until browned. Serve with mustard, if desired. Makes 5 servings.

Danish Ground Steak and Onion Sandwich (Hakkebøf)

Sweet, buttery onions and a delicate creamy sauce cap these patties.

¼ cup (⅛ lb.) butter or margarine
4 medium-sized onions, thinly sliced
  Salt
1½ pounds lean ground beef
  White pepper or finely ground black pepper
  All-purpose flour
1 tablespoon each butter and salad oil
3 English muffins, split, buttered, and toasted
½ cup whipping cream
½ teaspoon Worcestershire
  Chopped parsley for garnish

In a 10-inch frying pan over medium heat, melt the ¼ cup butter. Put in onions and cook slowly, stirring occasionally, until onions are limp and tinged with golden brown (this takes 20 to 25 minutes); stir in ½ teaspoon salt about halfway through the cooking. Transfer onions to a bowl and keep warm.

Meanwhile, shape ground beef into 6 patties, ½ to ¾ inch thick. Sprinkle lightly with salt and pepper, then coat with flour, shaking off excess. In the frying pan over medium-high heat, heat the 1 tablespoon butter and oil until sizzling; add meat patties and cook until well browned, 4 to 5 minutes on each side for medium-rare or until done to your liking. Transfer patties to toasted muffin halves; keep warm. Discard fat from the pan drippings; add cream and Worcestershire to pan. Cook, stirring to loosen browned particles, until cream is bubbly and slightly thickened. Spoon onions evenly over each ground beef patty, then pour sauce over all. Sprinkle with chopped parsley. Makes 6 servings.

Opera Sandwich

Ooperavoileipä, or Opera Sandwich, is a Finnish version of the hamburger. It's a slice of toasted French bread topped with a grilled patty, which is topped with a fried egg.

 2 pounds lean ground beef
 ½ cup finely chopped onion
1½ teaspoons salt
 ¼ teaspoon pepper
 3 tablespoons butter or margarine
 6 thick slices French bread, buttered on both sides
 6 eggs

In a bowl, combine ground beef with onion, salt, and pepper; mix until ingredients are thoroughly blended. Divide mixture into 6 portions, shape each into an oval patty. Melt 1 tablespoon of the butter in a heavy frying pan, add meat patties, and cook over medium heat 4 to 5 minutes on each side for medium-rare or until done to your liking.

In another frying pan, toast bread over medium heat until golden on both sides; remove from pan and keep hot. Using the same pan melt the remaining 2 tablespoons butter; add eggs and fry until whites are set but yolks are still soft. Place a patty on each slice of toasted bread and top with a fried egg. Serve immediately. Makes 6 servings.

Sourdough Cheeseburger Slices

This giant cheeseburger is baked and served on a long sourdough bread loaf cut lengthwise.

 1 can (8 oz.) tomato sauce with cheese
 2 tablespoons Worcestershire
 1 teaspoon salt
 ⅛ teaspoon pepper
 ½ cup fine dry bread crumbs
 2 pounds lean ground beef
 ½ cup finely chopped onion
 2 tablespoons chopped parsley
 1 long loaf (about 1 lb.) brown and serve
    sourdough French bread
 6 ounces Cheddar cheese, sliced

Blend tomato sauce, Worcestershire, salt, and pepper. Stir in bread crumbs and let stand for several minutes. Lightly mix in ground beef, onion, and parsley. Cut bread in half lengthwise. Spread meat mixture evenly over cut faces of bread, covering to edges. Bake, crust sides down, on an ungreased baking sheet in a 400° oven for about 25 minutes or until meat is well browned.

Arrange cheese over meat during the last 3 minutes or so of baking to melt slightly. Cut each half loaf into 4 pieces to serve. Makes 8 sandwiches.

The Burger Minus the Bun

Cheeseburgers with Guacamole

For a light supper, accompany these beef patties with corn chips and a tossed green salad.

1½ pounds lean ground beef
 ½ teaspoon each garlic salt and onion salt
 1 teaspoon Worcestershire
1½ cups shredded sharp Cheddar cheese
 1 can (7¾ oz.) thawed frozen avocado dip
    or 1 avocado, peeled and mashed
 1 tablespoon lemon juice
 3 drops liquid hot pepper seasoning

(Continued on next page)

Mix together the ground beef, garlic salt, onion salt, and Worcestershire. Mix in the cheese. Shape into 4 patties about 1 inch thick. Broil about 4 inches from heat 4 to 5 minutes on each side for medium-rare or until done to your liking.

Mix together the avocado dip or mashed avocado, lemon juice, and hot pepper seasoning. Spoon on top of each patty. Makes 4 servings.

Celery Stalks the Burger

Lightly sautéed celery and bean sprouts fill these moist beef patties.

    1 tablespoon butter or margarine
    ½ cup finely chopped celery stalks and leaves
    ½ cup fresh bean sprouts, coarsely chopped
    2 pounds lean ground beef
    1 teaspoon salt
    ¼ teaspoon ground cumin seed
    ⅛ teaspoon pepper
    1 egg

In a frying pan over medium-high heat melt the butter and sauté celery and bean sprouts for 2 to 3 minutes. Set pan aside.

To the ground beef, add salt, cumin, pepper, and egg and mix lightly. Form the meat mixture into 6 balls, poke a well in each and fill with about 2 tablespoons of the celery mixture. Close the hole, squash the balls into flat patties, and cook on a grill about 6 inches above hot coals 3 to 4 minutes per side for rare or until done to your liking. Makes 6 servings.

Korean Hamburgers

If you can buy toasted sesame seed, use it. Otherwise sprinkle regular sesame seed in a wide heavy pan and place over medium-high heat until golden, stirring constantly.

    1 pound lean ground beef
    2 tablespoons soy sauce
      Dash pepper
    1 small clove garlic, mashed
    1 green onion, chopped
    1 tablespoon toasted sesame seed
      About 3 tablespoons all-purpose flour
    1 egg, beaten with 1 tablespoon water
    1 to 2 tablespoons salad oil
      Dipping Sauce (recipe follows)

In a bowl combine the ground beef, soy sauce, pepper, garlic, green onion, and sesame seed. Cover and refrigerate if made ahead.

Shape the meat into 12 to 16 small patties, then dredge each in flour to coat lightly all over. Dip each patty into the beaten egg to coat, then set on a cake rack to drain briefly.

Heat a heavy 10-inch frying pan over medium heat. Put in salad oil, then the meat. Cook until browned (about 2 minutes on each side). Remove patties to a serving plate, cover, and set in a 150° oven for up to 1 hour. Serve with Dipping Sauce. Makes about 4 servings.

Dipping Sauce. Combine 4 tablespoons soy sauce with 4 teaspoons vinegar; blend in 2 teaspoons honey or firmly packed brown sugar, and a dash of liquid hot pepper seasoning. If desired, stir in 2 teaspoons toasted sesame seed or finely chopped green onion.

Smoky Ground Beef Cakes

Liquid smoke and bacon give a charcoal fire flavor to broiled ground beef patties.

    1½ pounds lean ground beef
      1 egg
    ½ cup finely chopped onion
      1 teaspoon salt
    ½ teaspoon pepper
      1 teaspoon rubbed sage
    1½ teaspoons liquid smoke
      6 slices bacon

Combine the ground beef with the egg, onion, salt, pepper, sage, and liquid smoke; shape into

6 thick cakes. Wrap one slice of bacon around the outside of each patty and secure with a toothpick; chill. Broil about 4 inches from heat 4 to 5 minutes on each side for medium-rare or until done to your liking. Makes 6 servings.

Teriyaki Turkey Patties

These well seasoned patties cook quickly on top of the range or under the broiler.

1½ pounds ground turkey
 ¼ cup fine dry bread crumbs
 1 egg
 2 tablespoons each finely chopped mushrooms
     and green onions, including part of the tops
 2 cloves garlic, minced or mashed
1½ teaspoons ground ginger
2½ tablespoons soy sauce
     Salad oil

Mix together the turkey, crumbs, egg, mushrooms, green onions, garlic, ginger, and soy sauce. Divide the mixture into 6 equal-sized portions and shape into patties about ½ inch thick. If you sauté the patties, heat 2 tablespoons oil in a 12-inch frying pan over medium-low heat for 1 minute. Lay the patties in the pan and cook about 5 minutes on each side or until meat is no longer pink inside. Or, if you broil the patties, place them on a broiler pan about 4 inches from the heat and cook 4 to 5 minutes on each side or until meat is no longer pink inside. Makes 6 servings.

Turkey Bacon Logs

The bacon wrapping keeps these lean ground turkey logs moist and juicy.

 1 pound ground turkey
 ¼ cup fine dry bread crumbs
 1 egg
 ¼ cup each minced parsley and green onion,
     including part of tops
 ¼ teaspoon each salt and pepper
 8 slices bacon (about ½ lb.)

In a bowl combine the ground turkey, bread crumbs, egg, parsley, green onion, salt, and pepper. Mix until blended. Divide mixture into 8 equal portions and shape each in a 2-inch-long log. Wrap each log with one slice bacon, securing end with a toothpick. Place on a rack in a broiler

pan. Bake in a 425° oven until bacon is brown and crisp (about 40 minutes). Makes 4 servings.

Cheese-Crusted Veal Patties

Veal patties, flavored with Parmesan cheese, stay moist inside, while the crumb and cheese coating fries crisp on the outside.

 1 pound lean ground veal
 ½ cup each fine dry bread crumbs and grated
     Parmesan cheese
 2 eggs
 ½ teaspoon salt
 ¼ teaspoon pepper
 ⅛ teaspoon garlic powder
 2 tablespoons each dry white wine and finely
     chopped green onion, including part of the tops
     About ⅓ cup all-purpose flour
 2 tablespoons salad oil

Mix together the veal, ¼ cup each of the bread crumbs and cheese, 1 of the eggs, salt, pepper, garlic powder, wine, and onion. Divide into 4 equal-sized portions and shape into patties about ½-inch thick.

In a small dish mix together the remaining ¼ cup each bread crumbs and cheese. In 2 other dishes have ready the flour and remaining egg, beaten. Coat each patty with flour, shaking off excess; dip in the egg to cover; then coat all sides with the crumb mixture. Heat the salad oil in a 10-inch frying pan over medium-low heat for 1 minute. Then lay the patties in the pan and cook 5 minutes on each side or until meat is no longer pink inside. Makes 4 servings.

Mexican Hamburgers

Colorful elements of a taco—guacamole, red peppers, jack cheese, and green onions—enliven these cumin-flavored hamburger patties.

1½ pounds lean ground beef
½ teaspoon each salt, garlic salt, and ground cumin seed
¼ pound jack cheese, shredded
  Guacamole (recipe follows)
2 green onions, sliced
4 canned, pickled hot red chile peppers
1 lime, cut in wedges
  Shredded iceberg lettuce
  Corn chips for garnish

Mix ground beef with salt, garlic salt, and cumin; shape into 4 patties about ¾ inch thick. Place on a broiling rack and broil about 4 inches from heat, turning once, about 4 to 5 minutes on each side for medium-rare or until done to your liking. Arrange patties on a serving platter or individual plates. Sprinkle each patty with cheese, add a spoonful of guacamole, sprinkle lightly with onions, and top with a red pepper. Garnish with a lime wedge. Make a ring of shredded lettuce around each patty and serve with corn chips. Makes 4 servings.

Guacamole. Cut 1 medium-sized avocado in half, remove seed, scoop out meat, and place in a small bowl. Mash with a fork; blend in 3 tablespoons lemon juice, ¼ teaspoon each salt, garlic salt, and ground cumin seed, and 2 canned California green chiles, seeded and finely chopped.

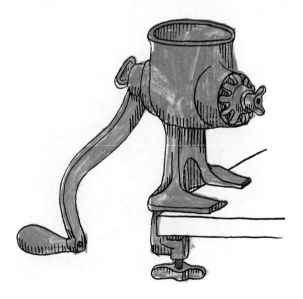

Grilled Lamb Patties

Barbecue these raisin-studded lamb patties and serve with a chutney-yogurt sauce.

1 pound lean ground lamb
¼ cup each finely chopped onion and fine dry bread crumbs
1 egg
⅓ cup raisins
½ teaspoon each garlic salt and curry powder
¼ teaspoon ground cinnamon
⅛ teaspoon each ground nutmeg and pepper
  Unflavored yogurt
  Major Grey's chutney, finely chopped

Combine the ground lamb, onion, bread crumbs, egg, raisins, garlic salt, curry powder, cinnamon, nutmeg, and pepper. Divide into 4 equal-sized portions; shape each into a patty ½ to ¾ inches thick.

Cook patties on a barbecue grill about 4 inches above a bed of medium-hot glowing coals about 6 minutes; turn and cook 6 minutes longer or until inside is no longer pink when slashed. Served with a bowl of unflavored yogurt seasoned to taste with finely chopped Major Grey's chutney. Makes 4 servings.

Spicy Pork Patties

These pork patties taste much like Italian sausages. Try serving them with hot garlic bread and a mixed green salad.

1 pound lean ground pork
¼ cup fine dry bread crumbs
1 egg
2 cloves garlic, minced or mashed
2 tablespoons dry red wine
½ teaspoon each salt, pepper, and fennel or anise seed
  Salad oil

Mix together the pork, crumbs, egg, garlic, wine, salt, pepper, and fennel seed. Divide into 4 equal-sized portions and shape into patties about ½ inch thick. If you sauté the patties heat 1 tablespoon salad oil in a 10-inch frying pan over medium-low heat for 1 minute. Lay the patties in the pan and cook 6 to 7 minutes on each side or until meat is no longer pink inside. Or, if you broil the patties, place them on a broiler rack about 4 inches from the heat and cook about 6 minutes on each side or until meat loses pinkness. Makes 4 servings.

Homemade Hamburger Relish

Make any of these relishes when the vegetables are in good supply; then enjoy their fresh flavor on hamburgers or frankfurters year-around.

Here are three distinct relish tastes to please different palates. Long, slow cooking concentrates the spicy ginger flavor of the Tomato Relish. The colorful Zucchini Relish is crisp and tart. The Cucumber Relish is spicy sweet.

Have the canning kettle half-filled with *hot* (not boiling) water. Scald the lids with boiling water and have more boiling water handy. The jars should be clean and hot. Ladle boiling hot relish into jars to within ¼ inch of the top. Slide a spatula between jar and relish to release air bubbles; carefully wipe jar rim with a clean, damp cloth; set on lid and screw on ring band.

As each jar is filled, set on a rack in the kettle. When all are filled, add boiling water to cover jars with an inch of water. Cover kettle, turn heat to high, and, when water boils, start counting processing time. Process 15 minutes for half-pints or pints of these relishes. Remove jars and cool on a cloth or board.

Tomato Relish

    8 *pounds tomatoes (about 16)*
      Boiling water
    3 *large onions, chopped*
    5 *large green apples, peeled, cored,*
      and sliced
    3 *whole lemons, thinly sliced*
    4 *tablespoons (about 5 oz.) grated*
      fresh ginger
    3 *cloves garlic, minced or mashed*
    ½ *cup sugar*
    1 *tablespoon salt*
    2 *tablespoons whole mustard seed*
    1 *teaspoon ground cloves*
    ¼ *teaspoon cayenne*
    1½ *cups each white wine vinegar and honey*

Dip tomatoes in rapidly boiling water for about 20 seconds, then rinse in cold water and peel; cut out stem ends.

In a kettle (about 12-quart size) combine tomatoes, onions, apples, lemons, ginger, garlic, sugar, salt, mustard seed, cloves, cayenne, vinegar, and honey; bring to boiling. Reduce heat and simmer gently, uncovered, for about 6 hours or until reduced to about 7 pints; stir often during last hour.

Zucchini Relish

    5 *pounds zucchini (about 20*
      medium-sized)
    6 *large onions*
    ½ *cup salt*
      Cold water
    2 *cups white wine vinegar*
    1 *cup sugar*
    1 *teaspoon dry mustard*
    2 *teaspoons celery seed*
    ½ *teaspoon each ground cinnamon, nutmeg,*
      and pepper
    2 *jars (4 oz. each) pimientos, drained*
      and chopped

Put zucchini and onions through the medium blade of a food chopper or finely chop with a knife; mix with salt in a bowl and cover with water. Cover and refrigerate for 4 hours or overnight.

Drain vegetables, rinse, then drain again. In a 5 or 6-quart pan, combine vegetables, vinegar, sugar, dry mustard, celery seed, cinnamon, nutmeg, pepper, and pimientos. Bring quickly to boiling, stirring constantly. Reduce heat and simmer, uncovered, for about 20 minutes or until reduced to about 6 pints. Stir occasionally.

Cucumber Relish

    12 *large cucumbers, peeled*
     4 *large onions*
     6 *green peppers, stems and seeds removed*
     4 *teaspoons each celery seed and*
       mustard seed
     1 *teaspoon salt*
     ½ *teaspoon ground cloves*
     1 *tablespoon ground turmeric*
    3½ *cups cider vinegar*
    2½ *cups sugar*

Put cucumbers, onions, and green peppers through the medium blade of a food chopper or finely chop with a knife. In a 5 or 6-quart pan, combine vegetables, celery seed, mustard seed, salt, cloves, turmeric, vinegar, and sugar. Quickly bring to boiling, stirring constantly; reduce heat and simmer, uncovered, for about 3 hours or until reduced to about 5 pints. Stir occasionally.

Ground Beef Patties with Lemon Glaze

You brown the meat patties first then simmer them briefly in a lemon sauce.

1½ pounds lean ground beef
2 tablespoons finely chopped onion
½ teaspoon salt
1 teaspoon grated lemon peel
1 egg
1 tablespoon salad oil
2 tablespoons vinegar
½ teaspoon ground ginger
3 tablespoons firmly packed brown sugar
1 bay leaf
6 thin slices from whole lemon
2 beef bouillon cubes

In a bowl combine the ground beef, onion, salt, lemon peel, and egg. Mix lightly and shape into 6 thick patties. In a frying pan heat the oil over medium-high heat; add the meat patties and brown well on both sides. Remove patties and set aside; discard any fat in pan. To the pan add the vinegar, ginger, brown sugar, bay leaf, lemon slices, and bouillon cubes. Bring to a boil, return patties to pan, reduce heat, cover, and simmer until meat is done to your liking (about 8 minutes for medium-well), turning once or twice. Serve patties with lemon glaze spooned evenly over top. Makes 6 servings.

Barbecued Hamburger Cups

You can make these individual hamburger cups by molding the ground beef mixture over the outside of foil muffin cups. For the cups, buy foil muffin pans, use kitchen scissors to cut cups apart, and trim the edges.

1½ pounds lean ground beef
1 egg
3 tablespoons fine dry bread crumbs
½ teaspoon salt
¼ teaspoon pepper
    Sautéed Mushrooms (recipe follows)
½ cup shredded Cheddar cheese

Mix together the ground beef, egg, dry bread crumbs, salt, and pepper. Divide meat mixture into 6 equal portions, forming each portion into a patty about ½ inch thick and 4 inches in diameter. Mold each patty evenly over the outside of a muffin cup. Place on a barbecue grill, 4 to 6 inches above glowing coals, with the inside of the muffin cup facing down.

Cook until bottom edges are browned and the top part of the mound is still slightly pink. (Meat next to cup should be cooked enough that it will hold the shape of a cup when turned.) Turn; remove foil cups carefully. Fill meat cups with the Sautéed Mushrooms; top each evenly with the shredded cheese; cook only until cheese melts. Makes 6 servings.

Sautéed Mushrooms. In a small pan, melt 2 tablespoons butter or margarine over medium-low heat. Add 1 tablespoon *each* chopped green onion and chopped parsley, ½ pound mushrooms (quartered), ¼ teaspoon salt, and ⅛ teaspoon pepper. Cook slowly until mushrooms are golden brown (5 to 8 minutes), stirring occasionally.

Teriyaki Beef Patties

Serve these patties with hot steamed rice and a green salad.

2 pounds lean ground beef
1 tablespoon salad oil
¼ pound mushrooms, sliced
⅓ cup each prepared teriyaki sauce and water
2 teaspoons each cornstarch and water
    Plain or toasted sesame seed

Shape the ground beef into 4 thick round patties. Heat salad oil in a large frying pan over medium-high heat; sauté meat on each side until browned. Lift out meat, add mushrooms and sauté until golden. Drain any fat from pan, return meat, and add the teriyaki sauce and the ⅓ cup water. Cover and simmer gently for about 10 minutes or until beef is medium-rare; remove to warm serving dish. Blend the cornstarch with the 2 teaspoons water and add to pan juices. Cook, stirring, until thickened. Pour sauce over beef and sprinkle with sesame seed. Makes 4 servings.

Orange Lamb Patties

Orange and coriander flavor these lamb patties. Serve them with rice and a cucumber salad.

1½ pounds lean ground lamb
¼ cup fine dry bread crumbs
1 egg
1½ teaspoons ground coriander
½ teaspoon grated orange peel
¼ cup orange juice
2 tablespoons soy sauce
Salad oil

Mix together the lamb, crumbs, egg, coriander, orange peel, orange juice, and soy. Divide the mixture into 6 equal-sized portions and shape into patties about ½ inch thick. If you sauté the patties, heat 2 tablespoons salad oil in a 12-inch frying pan over medium-low heat for 1 minute. Lay patties in the pan and cook 5 to 6 minutes on each side for medium-well done. Or, if you broil the patties, place them on a broiler pan about 4 inches from the heat and cook about 5 minutes on each side for medium-well done. Makes 6 servings.

Hamburger Steak, Soubise

Cook this giant hamburger on top of the range for a few minutes, then brown the top under the broiler.

4 tablespoons butter or margarine
3 medium-sized onions, thinly sliced
1½ cups boiling water
2 pounds lean ground beef
1 teaspoon salt
Dash pepper
⅛ teaspoon garlic salt
¼ teaspoon smoke-flavored salt
1 cup sour cream
Parsley for garnish

Heat 3 tablespoons of the butter in a frying pan over medium heat and sauté onions about 5 minutes. Add boiling water and simmer, uncovered, for 20 minutes or until most of the liquid has cooked away. Meanwhile, combine the ground beef, salt, pepper, garlic salt, and smoke-flavored salt; mix until blended, then shape into one 8-inch patty. Melt the remaining 1 tablespoon butter in an 8-inch cake pan. Fit the meat patty into the pan. Cook on top of range over medium heat for about 5 minutes or until nicely browned on bottom. Set into a preheated broiler about 3 inches below heat and broil about 6 minutes for meat cooked rare, a few minutes longer for medium-well done. With a slotted spatula transfer meat to a rimmed platter.

Add sour cream to onion mixture; stir over medium heat just until heated—do not boil. Pour sauce over meat and cut in wedges to serve. Garnish with sprigs of parsley. Makes 4 to 6 servings.

Build a Better Meatball

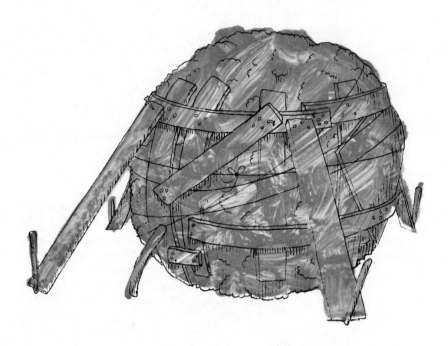

Gig Harbor Meatballs

These meatballs are exceptionally moist and light because of the unusual binding ingredients: mashed potatoes and rolled oats.

        Instant mashed potatoes
    4 pounds lean ground beef
    1 envelope (about 1⅜ oz.) onion soup mix
           (enough for 3 or 4 servings)
    4 eggs
    1 cup milk
    ½ cup quick-cooking rolled oats
    ⅓ cup finely chopped parsley
    ¾ teaspoon ground nutmeg
    ¼ cup each butter or margarine and
           all-purpose flour
    1 pint (2 cups) milk or half-and-half (light cream)
    1 teaspoon salt
    ½ pint (1 cup) sour cream

Prepare enough instant mashed potatoes to make 1 cup, adding water, milk, and seasonings as directed on the package. Using a heavy-duty electric mixer or your hands, mix together the ground beef, onion soup mix, eggs, the 1 cup milk, mashed potatoes, rolled oats, parsley, and

½ teaspoon of the nutmeg. Mix until smoothly blended. Shape into 1¼-inch balls and place 1 inch apart on shallow baking pans. Bake, uncovered, in a 450° oven for 10 minutes or until well browned. Transfer to a 3 to 3½-quart casserole, reserving the pan drippings.

For the sour cream gravy, melt butter in a saucepan over medium heat until bubbly and blend in flour; cook a few minutes until flour mixture turns golden brown. Gradually stir in the 2 cups milk and, stirring constantly, cook until thickened. Add reserved drippings, salt, remaining ¼ teaspoon nutmeg, and sour cream, stirring to blend.

Spoon sauce over meatballs. At this point you may let cool to room temperature, cover, and refrigerate until serving time (as long as a day ahead). Or bake immediately without cooling. Bake in a 350° oven, uncovered, for about 25 minutes (35 minutes if refrigerated) or until hot through. Makes 12 to 16 servings.

Freezer note. If you like, you can make meatballs ahead and freeze them without the sauce. Package drippings at the same time and freeze separately. To serve, let meatballs and drippings thaw. Then make sauce with drippings, spoon over meatballs, and reheat in a 350° oven for 35 minutes.

Greek Meatballs Oregano

As an authentic accompaniment, you might like to serve Greek wines and ouzo, the potent anise-flavored liqueur.

6 *slices firm white bread, crumbled*
1 *cup milk*
1 *cup finely chopped onion*
2 *tablespoons butter or margarine*
4 *pounds lean ground beef*
¾ *cup finely chopped parsley*
4 *egg yolks*
3 *teaspoons salt*
¼ *teaspoon pepper*
¾ *cup red wine vinegar*
1 *teaspoon oregano leaves*

Soak the crumbled bread in the milk for 5 minutes; beat with a fork until mushy. In a frying pan over medium heat, sauté the chopped onion in butter until golden. In a large mixing bowl place the ground beef, parsley, egg yolks, the milk mixture, sautéed onions, salt, and pepper. Thoroughly mix with your hands. Shape in 1¼-inch balls and place on rimmed baking pans. Bake, uncovered, in a 450° oven for 15 minutes or until meatballs are well-browned and slightly pink in the center.

Meanwhile, bring the vinegar and oregano to a boil, reduce heat, and let simmer, uncovered, 10 minutes; pour evenly over hot meatballs in each pan, scraping up the pan juices. Serve immediately or leave in pan and chill, covered, or freeze. To serve later (thaw if frozen), heat in a 375° oven for 15 minutes. Serve warm. Makes about 6 dozen meatballs.

Ground Beef Curry Balls

Canned beef broth is the seasoning shortcut to this quick curry sauce.

1 *large onion, finely chopped*
1 *tablespoon salad oil or olive oil*
1½ *pounds lean ground beef*
1 *tablespoon curry powder*
1 *can (14 oz.) regular strength beef broth*
2 *teaspoons cornstarch*
1 *tablespoon lemon juice*
  Salt and pepper
3 *to 4 cups hot steamed rice*
  Assorted condiments (suggestions follow)

Using a large frying pan, sauté onion in oil over medium heat until golden; push to the sides of the pan. Quickly shape meat into bite-sized balls and drop into the pan; brown on all sides. Add curry powder and sauté 1 minute. Blend 2 tablespoons of the broth with the cornstarch to make a paste; pour remaining broth into pan and bring to a boil. Stir in cornstarch paste and cook, stirring gently, until thickened; stir in lemon juice, and salt and pepper to taste. Turn curried meat into a hot serving bowl. Mound rice in another bowl. Serve at the table with assorted condiments (see below). Makes 4 to 6 servings.

Assorted Condiments. Place in individual bowls ¾ cup flaked coconut; ¾ cup salted cashews, chopped; 1 small cucumber, chopped; and 1 can (about 9 oz.) pineapple tidbits, drained.

Curried Lamb Meatballs with Fruit

Fruit flavors complement the spicy seasoning in this attractive curry entrée.

1½ *pounds lean ground lamb*
1 *egg*
3 *tablespoons fine dry bread crumbs*
1 *teaspoon salt*
2 *tablespoons salad oil*
1 *medium-sized onion, finely chopped*
2 *cloves garlic, minced or mashed*
1 *tablespoon curry powder*
1 *can (14½ oz.) sliced tomatoes, drained*
1 *apple, peeled and diced*
2 *tablespoons red wine vinegar*
1 *tablespoon apricot jam*
2 *green-tipped bananas*
1 *tablespoon butter or margarine*
  Hot steamed rice (about 3 cups)

For meatballs, mix together the ground meat, egg, crumbs, and salt; shape into 1¼-inch balls. Heat oil in a large frying pan over medium-high heat, add meatballs, and sauté until browned on all sides, turning frequently. Push to the sides of the pan. Add onion and garlic and sauté for 3 to 4 minutes. Add curry powder and sauté 1 minute, stirring. Stir in tomatoes, apple, vinegar, and jam. Cover and simmer 30 minutes.

(Continued on next page)

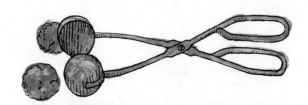

Peel and slice bananas on the diagonal. In another pan, over medium-high heat, quickly sauté the bananas in butter on all sides, just until glazed. Mound rice in the center of a rimmed serving plate and surround with meatballs and sauce. Garnish with sautéed bananas. Serves 6.

Beef-Wheat Balls

Quick cooking cracked wheat and chopped walnuts give a crunchy texture to these herb seasoned meatballs.

1 *pound lean ground beef*
¾ *cup quick cooking cracked wheat (bulgur)*
½ *cup finely chopped onion*
½ *teaspoon salt*
2 *tablespoons minced parsley*
¼ *teaspoon each thyme and marjoram leaves*
⅛ *teaspoon basil leaves*
2 *tablespoons chopped walnuts*
2 *cans (10½ oz. each) condensed beef bouillon*
2 *soup cans water*
1½ *cups sour cream with chives*
   Hot buttered noodles or rice

Mix together ground beef, cracked wheat, onion, salt, parsley, thyme, marjoram, basil, and nuts. Roll into balls the size of small walnuts. In a large kettle, bring to a boil the beef bouillon and water; drop in meatballs, cover and simmer until balls rise to top (about 15 minutes). Remove meatballs from broth and mix them with sour cream; reserve broth for other uses. Serve meatballs over hot buttered noodles or rice. Makes about 4 servings.

Bacon Meatballs

For a more colorful entrée sprinkle chopped onion or minced parsley over the meatballs just before you serve.

2 *cups milk*
1 *cup soft crumbs of sour French bread or rolls,*
   lightly packed
6 *slices bacon*
1 *pound lean ground beef*
1 *egg*
½ *teaspoon salt*
   Dash pepper
1 *tablespoon all-purpose flour*
¼ *teaspoon oregano leaves*
   Hot cooked green noodles or brown rice

Pour ⅔ cup of the milk over crumbs and let stand until milk is absorbed. In a large frying pan over medium heat, cook bacon until crisp; crumble and set aside. Discard all but 1 tablespoon of the drippings. To the bread and milk mixture, add the ground beef, egg, salt, pepper, and crumbled bacon. Mix lightly until blended and form into balls about the size of golf balls. Sauté meatballs in the 1 tablespoon bacon drippings, over medium heat, turning until browned on all sides. Remove meat from pan and stir in flour and oregano; cook, stirring, until bubbly. Remove from heat and gradually stir in the remaining 1⅓ cups milk. Cook, stirring, until bubbly; return meatballs to pan. Cover, reduce heat, and simmer, stirring occasionally, about 15 minutes or until meat has lost all pinkness when slashed. Serve over hot green noodles or brown rice. Makes about 4 servings.

Skewered Pork Balls with Apple

Savory pork balls and apple quarters are skewered with bacon in between.

1½ *pounds lean ground pork*
1 *egg*
⅓ *cup each fine dry bread crumbs and finely*
   chopped onion
2 *tablespoons apple juice*
½ *teaspoon each salt and ground ginger*
¼ *teaspoon each ground sage and pepper*
8 *slices bacon*
2 *Golden Delicious apples, quartered, core*
   removed, and peeled, if desired
   Sweet pickle relish

Combine the ground pork, egg, bread crumbs, onion, apple juice, salt, ginger, sage, and pepper. Divide into 16 equal-sized portions; shape each into a ball; set aside.

To assemble the skewers (you'll need 4), pierce one end of a bacon strip with a skewer, then push on a pork ball, pierce the bacon again, and add an apple quarter. Pierce bacon again, push on another pork ball, and then pierce the bacon end; the bacon forms S-curves around the meat and apple. Repeat the procedure until each skewer has 2 bacon strips, 4 pork balls, and 2 apple quarters; space elements loosely so bacon will brown evenly.

Cook on a grill about 6 inches above a solid bed of low glowing coals. Turn gently (with the help of a wide spatula) as needed to brown evenly until bacon is crisp and pork is no longer pink inside (15 to 20 minutes total). Pass sweet pickle relish as an accompaniment. Makes 4 servings.

Turkish Meatballs on Skewers

The refreshing tang of yogurt or sour cream complements these mint-flavored Turkish meatballs.

 2 medium-sized green peppers
   Boiling salted water
 1 pound lean ground lamb
 1 pound lean ground beef
 ¼ cup each fine dry bread crumbs, chopped onion, and parsley
 2 eggs
 1 tablespoon crumbled dried mint leaves
 1¼ teaspoons salt
 ¼ teaspoon pepper
   Olive oil
   Quick-cooking cracked wheat (bulgur), prepared according to package directions
   Unflavored yogurt or sour cream

Cut peppers into 24 pieces about 1 to 1½ inches square, removing any seeds. Drop into boiling salted water and boil 1 minute. Drain immediately; set aside.

In a large bowl, combine lamb, beef, crumbs, onion, parsley, eggs, mint, salt, and pepper. Mix well and form into 30 balls, each about the size of a golf ball. Alternately, thread 5 meatballs and 4 pepper squares on each of 6 skewers. Place on the rack of a broiler pan, brush with olive oil, and cook in a preheated broiler about 4 inches from heat for about 8 minutes or until meat is done to your liking, turning to brown all sides. To serve, arrange skewers on a bed of cooked cracked wheat and pass yogurt in a separate dish. Serves 6.

Indian Lamb Kebabs

Serve these ground lamb balls as an entrée for dinner with fruit chutney, a green salad, and a rice pilaf.

 1 pound lean ground lamb
 1 medium-sized onion, finely chopped
 2 cloves garlic, minced or mashed
 2 tablespoons chopped parsley
 ¼ cup fine dry bread crumbs
 1 egg
 ¼ teaspoon cayenne
 2 teaspoons ground coriander
 ½ teaspoon each ground cumin seed, turmeric, and ginger
 1 teaspoon salt

In a large bowl, mix together thoroughly the lamb, onion, garlic, parsley, bread crumbs, egg, cayenne, coriander, cumin, turmeric, ginger, and salt.

Divide mixture into 12 equal portions, roll each into a thin cylinder about 6 inches long, and string on a skewer. With your hands, press meat securely over each skewer to form a smooth sausage; place on broiler pan. Broil 4 inches from heat for 6 to 8 minutes, turning once, until meat is well browned and done to your liking. Makes 3 to 4 servings.

Add meatballs, bring to a boil, reduce heat, cover, and simmer about 5 minutes or until zucchini is tender. Stir cornstarch and water mixture into sauce and cook, stirring, until sauce is thickened. Serve immediately over cooked rice or pasta. Makes about 6 servings.

Oriental Meatball Dinner

If you cook the meat ahead, this dish can be quickly assembled at dinner time.

    1 pound lean ground beef
1½ pounds lean ground pork
    1 can (5 oz.) water chestnuts, drained
        and chopped
    2 eggs, slightly beaten
  ⅔ cup quick-cooking rolled oats
  ⅓ cup chopped onion
    1 teaspoon ground ginger
1½ teaspoons salt
    1 can (14 oz.) regular strength beef broth
    1 tablespoon sesame seed
    2 tablespoons salad oil
    1 medium-sized green pepper, seeded and cut
        in strips
    2 cups sliced zucchini (about 3 small zucchini)
    1 medium-sized onion, sliced
    4 stalks celery, diagonally sliced
    4 cloves garlic, minced or mashed
  ⅔ cup water
  ¼ cup soy sauce
    3 tablespoons cornstarch
    4 cups hot cooked rice

In a large bowl, thoroughly combine with your hands the beef, pork, water chestnuts, eggs, rolled oats, chopped onion, ginger, salt, ⅔ cup of the beef broth, and sesame seed. Shape into smooth balls, using 2 tablespoons mixture for each.

Place meatballs slightly apart on ungreased rimmed baking sheets. Bake in a 450° oven for 30 minutes or until meat is lightly browned and the interior has lost all pinkness. Use hot (or chill, covered, as long as overnight, then reheat for 10 minutes in a 350° oven before continuing).

Pour salad oil into a large frying pan. Place over medium heat; add green pepper, zucchini, sliced onion, celery, and garlic; cook, stirring, for about 3 minutes or until vegetables are tender-crisp.

Add hot meatballs, remaining broth, and water; bring to a simmer. Blend soy sauce with cornstarch until smooth; add to meat mixture, stirring briskly to distribute. Cook, stirring, until sauce is thickened and clear. To serve, spoon meatballs and sauce over rice. Serves 8.

Zesty Zucchini

A variety of garden vegetables turn these meatballs into a colorful, richly flavored, one-dish meal.

    2 pounds lean ground beef
        Salt and pepper
    2 tablespoons salad oil
    2 stalks celery, thinly sliced
    1 large onion, diced
    1 medium-sized green pepper, seeded and diced
  ¼ pound mushrooms, sliced
    1 clove garlic, minced or mashed
    3 medium-sized zucchini, thinly sliced
    1 can (1 lb. 12 oz.) whole tomatoes
    2 tablespoons fresh lime juice
  ½ teaspoon each ground cumin seed and
        basil leaves
    1 teaspoon oregano leaves
    3 teaspoons cornstarch blended with ¼ cup
        cold water
        Hot cooked rice or pasta

Season ground beef with salt and pepper; shape into tiny meatballs, using about 1 tablespoon meat for each. Brown quickly over high heat in the oil in a large frying pan. Set meatballs aside. Discard all but 2 tablespoons of the pan drippings.

To the frying pan, add the celery, onion, green pepper, mushrooms, and garlic. Cook over medium heat, stirring, until onion is limp. Add zucchini, tomatoes and their liquid (break up tomatoes), lime juice, cumin, basil, oregano, and salt and pepper to taste.

Sweet-Sour Beef and Cabbage

The usual ingredients found in stuffed cabbage rolls are more simply combined here in this top-of-the-range entrée.

    1 pound lean ground beef
    ¼ cup soft bread crumbs
    1 egg, slightly beaten
    ½ medium-sized onion, finely chopped
    ½ green pepper, seeded and chopped
    1 clove garlic, minced or mashed
    2 tablespoons chopped parsley
    1 teaspoon salt
    2 tablespoons salad oil
    1 head cabbage (about 2 lbs.)
      Sweet-Sour Sauce (recipe follows)

Combine in a bowl the meat, bread crumbs, egg, onion, green pepper, garlic, parsley, and salt. Mix with your hands until well blended, then shape into balls about golf ball size. Using a Dutch oven or similar pan, heat oil over medium heat and brown meatballs, turning to brown all sides. Drain off any fat. Remove core and cut cabbage into narrow wedges; arrange over the meat. Pour Sweet-Sour Sauce over the cabbage and meat, cover pan, reduce heat, and simmer gently for 15 minutes or until cabbage is tender. Makes 4 to 6 servings.

Sweet-Sour Sauce. Combine 2 cans (8 oz. *each*) tomato sauce with ¼ cup cider vinegar, ¼ cup firmly packed brown sugar, ½ teaspoon salt, and ¼ teaspoon pepper; stir until blended.

Meatballs and Artichokes

Each element of this dish is done in sequence in the same frying pan.

    1 can (about 7 oz.) artichoke bottoms, drained
    1 pound lean ground beef
    1 large onion, finely chopped
    ¼ cup minced parsley
    ⅓ cup fine dry bread crumbs
    1 egg
      About 2 tablespoons butter or margarine
    2 tablespoons pine nuts
    1 tablespoon all-purpose flour
    ½ teaspoon each sugar and ground allspice
    ½ cup sour cream
    1 can (about 10 oz.) condensed beef bouillon

Cut artichoke bottoms in quarters; rinse with water and drain well. In a bowl combine the ground beef, onion, parsley, bread crumbs, and egg. Mix with your hands until thoroughly blended. Shape meat mixture in 1¼-inch balls.

Melt 1 tablespoon of the butter in a large frying pan; add pine nuts and cook over medium heat, stirring, until golden. With a slotted spoon remove nuts from pan and set aside. Add 1 more tablespoon butter to the pan; put in artichokes and cook, turning in butter to coat all sides, for about 2 minutes. With a slotted spoon lift artichokes from pan and keep warm.

Add meatballs to frying pan and cook over medium-high heat, uncovered, until well browned on all sides (about 15 minutes). Remove with a slotted spoon and keep warm.

Reduce heat to medium. If necessary, add butter to pan to make 1 tablespoon fat. Stir flour, sugar, and allspice into fat in pan and cook until bubbly. Stir in sour cream until smooth; then gradually stir in beef bouillon until blended. Cook, stirring, until mixture comes to simmering. Return meatballs and artichokes to pan, stirring to coat with sauce. Cover and simmer to heat through (about 5 minutes). Transfer to a serving dish and sprinkle with toasted pine nuts. Makes 4 servings.

Ham Balls with Sweet Potatoes

A sweet crusty glaze forms on the potatoes and ham balls as they bake. If you have leftover baked ham, you can grind it to use in this recipe.

      1 egg
      ½ cup milk
    1½ cups soft bread crumbs
      2 cups ground cooked ham
      1 teaspoon dry mustard
      1 can (about 1 lb.) vacuum-packed whole
        sweet potatoes
      2 tablespoons melted butter
      ½ cup firmly packed brown sugar
      2 tablespoons vinegar

In a bowl beat the egg slightly. Stir in the milk, bread crumbs, ground ham, and ½ teaspoon of the mustard. Mix lightly until well blended, then shape into about 12 balls. Distribute balls in a greased shallow baking dish (about 9 inches square). Arrange the sweet potatoes between the ham balls in the dish.

Combine the melted butter, brown sugar, vinegar, and remaining ½ teaspoon mustard; drizzle over the ham and potatoes. Bake, uncovered, in a 375° oven for about 40 minutes or until richly glazed; baste twice with sauce in pan. Makes 4 servings.

Baked Meatballs in French Wine Sauce

For an easy dinner that can be prepared ahead of time, you can shape the meatballs and prepare the sauce. Chill both until dinner; then quickly bake the meatballs, heat the sauce, and serve over rice.

1½ *pounds lean ground beef*
⅓ *cup each milk and fine dry bread crumbs*
2 *teaspoons instant minced onion*
2 *eggs*
1 *teaspoon Worcestershire*
¾ *teaspoon salt*
⅛ *teaspoon pepper*
Hot cooked rice
French Wine Sauce (recipe follows)

In a bowl combine the ground beef, milk, bread crumbs, instant minced onion, eggs, Worcestershire, salt, and pepper. Mix together until blended; shape into balls, using about 2 tablespoons mixture for each. Place on a greased, rimmed baking pan, cover, and chill well.

When ready to bake, place cold meatballs in a 500° oven for about 12 minutes or until well browned and just slightly pink inside. Arrange the rice on a serving platter, top with meatballs, and pour the wine sauce evenly over all. Serves 4.

French Wine Sauce. In a frying pan, melt ¼ cup butter or margarine and add ½ pound mushrooms, cut in quarters. Stir over medium heat until mushrooms are golden. Pour in ¾ cup water, blend in 1 teaspoon beef stock base or 1 beef bouillon cube, and stir to dissolve. Then add ¾ cup dry red wine, 2 tablespoons catsup, 1 bay leaf, 1 can (8 oz.) tiny whole onions (drained), and 1 clove garlic (minced or mashed). Slowly blend ¼ cup cold water into 4 teaspoons cornstarch; gradually stir into pan. Cook, stirring, until mixture boils and thickens. Cover and chill. Reheat before serving.

Spur-of-the-Moment Stroganoff

This quickly prepared stroganoff is a good choice when unexpected company appears.

½ *pound mushrooms*
4 *tablespoons butter or margarine*
1 *medium-sized onion, finely chopped*
2 *pounds lean ground beef*
½ *teaspoon tarragon leaves, crumbled*
¼ *teaspoon each pepper and basil leaves*
2 *tablespoons all-purpose flour*
⅓ *cup canned tomato paste*
1 *can (10½ oz.) condensed beef consommé*
2 *teaspoons Worcestershire*
1 *tablespoon vinegar*
1 *cup sour cream*
Salt
Buttered French bread

Slice mushrooms and sauté in 2 tablespoons of the butter in a large frying pan over medium heat until golden brown; using a slotted spoon, lift out mushrooms and set aside. Add the remaining 2 tablespoons butter to pan and sauté onion until golden; push to sides of pan. Quickly shape meat into bite-sized balls and drop into pan; sauté, shaking pan to turn until browned on all sides. Sprinkle with tarragon, pepper, basil, and flour. Stir in the tomato paste, consommé, Worcestershire, and vinegar; cover, reduce heat, and simmer 10 minutes. Add mushrooms to meat, stir in sour cream and salt to taste; heat through but do not boil. Serve with hot buttered French bread. Makes about 6 servings.

Meatballs with Rice and Celery

Cream of asparagus soup gives color and rich flavor to this hearty one-dish meal.

     1 pound lean ground beef
     ½ cup rolled oats (regular or quick-cooking)
     ½ teaspoon each salt and celery salt
     ¼ teaspoon pepper
     1 teaspoon minced parsley
     3 tablespoons butter or margarine
     1 cup uncooked rice
  1½ cups sliced celery
     1 large onion, chopped
     1 can (6 or 8 oz.) mushroom stems and pieces
     2 cans (10¾ oz. each) cream of asparagus soup
     2 cups water

Mix together the ground beef, rolled oats, salt, celery salt, pepper, and parsley. Roll meat into balls the size of medium-sized walnuts. In a large frying pan over medium heat sauté meatballs until brown on all sides in the butter or margarine. Arrange half the browned meatballs in the bottom of a greased 3-quart casserole. Cover with the rice, celery, and onion, and top with the remaining meatballs. Combine the mushrooms and their liquid, soup, and water; pour over all. Cover and bake in a 350° oven for 1 hour or until liquid is absorbed and rice is tender. Makes 6 servings.

Spiced Lamb Meatballs

Ground lamb offers a pleasant change from the usual choices in economical meats, and its flavor readily accepts a range of lively spices.

     1 medium-sized onion, finely chopped
     1 clove garlic, minced
     1 inch piece fresh ginger, chopped (or ¼ teaspoon ground ginger)
     2 tablespoons olive oil or salad oil
  1½ teaspoons salt
     1 teaspoon each ground cumin seed, ground coriander, and curry powder
     1 can (8 oz.) tomato sauce
     1 cup water
     2 pounds lean ground lamb
     ¼ cup wheat germ
     2 eggs
     2 tablespoons finely chopped fresh coriander or parsley
     ½ teaspoon ground allspice
       Hot steamed rice (about 3 cups)

Using a Dutch oven, over medium heat, sauté the onion, garlic, and fresh ginger, if used, in oil until golden. Add ½ teaspoon of the salt, cumin, coriander, curry, and ground ginger if used; sauté 1 minute. Pour in the tomato sauce and water. Cover and simmer while shaping meatballs.

Mix together the ground lamb, wheat germ, eggs, and the remaining 1 teaspoon salt. Shape into 1¼-inch balls. Drop into the simmering sauce, cover, and simmer 20 minutes or until meatballs are no longer pink inside. Sprinkle with the fresh coriander and allspice. Serve on plates with rice alongside. Makes 6 servings.

Spinach Meatballs with Tomato Sauce

You might pass additional Parmesan cheese at the table to sprinkle over top.

     1 package (10 oz.) frozen chopped spinach
     1 medium-sized onion, finely chopped
     1 clove garlic, minced or mashed
  1½ pounds lean ground beef
     3 tablespoons each grated Parmesan cheese and fine dry bread crumbs
     1 egg, slightly beaten
     1 teaspoon salt
     ⅛ teaspoon pepper
     2 tablespoons each butter or margarine and all-purpose flour
     1 can (8 oz.) tomato sauce
     1 teaspoon Worcestershire
     1 cup water

Defrost spinach, drain by pressing through a wire strainer; chop finely. Combine spinach with onion, garlic, beef, cheese, bread crumbs, egg, salt, and pepper; mix until well blended. Form into balls about the size of golf balls and arrange in a single layer in a shallow rimmed baking pan. Put into a 500° oven for 7 to 9 minutes, or until well browned.

Meanwhile, melt butter in a large frying pan over medium heat; stir in flour and cook until bubbly. Gradually stir in the tomato sauce, Worcestershire, and water; cook, stirring, until thickened. Add the meatballs and their juices and cook, uncovered, until meatballs are heated through. Makes 4 to 6 servings.

Meatballs in Tangy Sauce

The unusual thing about these meatballs is the distinctive beer-flavored sauce.

    1 slice firm white bread
    ⅓ cup warm water
    2 pounds lean ground beef
    1 egg
    2 cloves garlic, finely chopped
    1 medium-sized onion, finely chopped
    2 tablespoons Worcestershire
    1 teaspoon salt
    ½ teaspoon pepper
    2 tablespoons olive oil or salad oil
    1 package onion soup mix (amount for 3 or
       4 servings)
    1 can (12 oz.) beer
    1 cup (½ pint) sour cream
      Hot cooked rice

In a bowl soak bread in water, then add the meat, egg, garlic, onion, Worcestershire, salt, and pepper. Blend well and form into about 30 balls. In a frying pan, heat the oil, add meatballs, and cook over medium heat until well browned on all sides. Drain off all drippings. Sprinkle onion soup mix over meatballs. Add beer; cover and simmer for 10 minutes. Add sour cream; heat, stirring, just until well blended and heated through. Serve with hot cooked rice. Makes 6 to 8 servings.

Baked Kotleti

Austrians have a special way of preparing meatballs. Their trick of folding stiffly beaten egg whites into the meat mixture results in a pleasingly light and tender meatball.

    3 pounds lean ground beef
    4 tablespoons soft butter or margarine
    2 teaspoons salt
    ½ teaspoon freshly ground pepper
    2 tablespoons minced parsley
    6 slices day-old bread
      Water
    4 eggs, separated
    3 tablespoons all-purpose flour
    1 can (10½ oz.) condensed beef consommé
    ⅓ cup sour cream

Combine the ground beef, 2 tablespoons softened butter, salt, pepper, and parsley. Soak bread in water, squeeze nearly dry, and tear up finely; add

to the meat mixture along with egg yolks; mix thoroughly. Whip egg whites until stiff, but not dry, and fold in, stirring with a fork. Form meat mixture into 2 dozen 2½-inch patties. In a frying pan over medium heat, sauté the meat in the remaining butter until browned on each side. Transfer to a 2-quart casserole. Discard all but 3 tablespoons of the drippings.

Stir flour into the reserved pan drippings and brown slightly, then stir in consommé; bring to a boil. Remove from heat, stir in sour cream, blending until smooth, and pour over the meatballs. Bake, covered, in a 350° oven for 25 minutes. Makes about 10 servings.

Hot Meatball Sandwiches

Serve these hearty meatball sandwiches, made in big round French rolls, with plenty of napkins handy.

    1½ pounds lean ground beef
    ½ pound lean ground pork
    2 eggs
    ½ cup each fine dry bread crumbs and grated
       Romano cheese
    ¼ cup chopped parsley
    ½ teaspoon salt
    1 package (1½ oz.) spaghetti sauce mix
       with mushrooms
    1 tablespoon butter or margarine
    1 can (8 oz.) tomato sauce
    ½ cup water
      Butter or margarine
    8 round French rolls
      Grated Romano cheese

Thoroughly mix the beef, pork, eggs, bread crumbs, the ½ cup cheese, parsley, salt, and half the dry sauce mix (about 2 tablespoons).

Using a rounded tablespoon for each, shape meat mixture into 1½-inch balls. Brown meatballs in the 1 tablespoon butter in a large frying pan over medium-high heat, shaking pan to brown meatballs on all sides. Remove meatballs from pan and keep warm. Discard fat.

In the same pan, prepare remaining sauce mix by blending it with tomato sauce and water; heat until bubbly. Return meatballs to pan, cover, and cook over low heat about 25 minutes. Split and butter rolls; wrap in foil and heat in a 350° oven about 15 minutes. Serve meatballs in rolls, allowing 5 to 6 meatballs and a spoonful of sauce for each. Sprinkle with additional cheese. Makes 8 sandwiches.

Mexican Meatballs

This meatball dish is spicy hot; if you prefer mildly seasoned meatballs, reduce the chile powder by a teaspoon.

1 pound lean ground beef
½ cup fine dry bread crumbs
2 medium-sized onions, finely chopped
3 cloves garlic, minced or mashed
1 teaspoon ground coriander
½ teaspoon salt
¼ teaspoon pepper
2 eggs, slightly beaten
1 can (1 lb.) tomatoes
1 can (8 oz.) tomato sauce
3 teaspoons chile powder
  Hot buttered noodles, rice, cracked wheat,
    or polenta

Mix together thoroughly the ground beef, bread crumbs, 1 of the chopped onions, 2 cloves of the garlic, coriander, salt, pepper, and eggs. Shape into balls about 1¼ inches in diameter. Into a 4 or 5-quart kettle with a tight-fitting cover, put the tomatoes, tomato sauce, the remaining onion, the remaining garlic clove, and chile powder;

cover and simmer for 5 minutes. Drop meatballs into the hot tomato sauce, cover, and simmer for 45 minutes. Serve over hot buttered noodles, rice, cracked wheat, or polenta. Makes 4 servings.

German Meatballs

These fluffy meatballs absorb some of the cream gravy as they simmer.

1½ pounds lean ground beef
½ pound lean ground pork
¼ cup finely chopped onion
1 egg
½ cup fine dry bread crumbs
2 cups half-and-half (light cream)
1 teaspoon salt
¼ teaspoon pepper
1½ teaspoon firmly packed brown sugar
½ teaspoon ground allspice
¼ teaspoon ground nutmeg
2 tablespoons butter or margarine
  Paprika

Combine ground beef, ground pork, and onion. Beat egg lightly and mix into the meat mixture with bread crumbs, 1 cup of the half-and-half, salt, pepper, brown sugar, allspice, and nutmeg. Shape into small balls 1¼ inches in diameter. In a frying pan brown meatballs, a few at a time, on all sides in butter over medium-high heat (this takes about 10 minutes). Drain off all drippings. Pour the remaining 1 cup half-and-half over meatballs; cover, and simmer gently for 15 minutes. Sprinkle with paprika before serving. Makes 6 to 8 servings.

For Cocktail Time: The Miniature Meatball

Teriyaki Meatballs

It's easy to make appetizers when you combine ground meat with Teriyaki Sauce.

1 pound lean ground beef
¼ cup fine dry bread crumbs
1 egg
2 tablespoons Teriyaki Sauce (recipe follows)
2 tablespoons milk

(Continued on next page)

Combine the ground beef, bread crumbs, egg, Teriyaki Sauce, and milk. Form into balls about 1 inch in diameter; then dip into the remaining sauce, drain briefly, and place slightly apart on a greased, rimmed baking pan. (Cover and chill if made ahead.) Bake, uncovered, in a 450° oven for 10 minutes or until meatballs are no longer pink inside. Offer picks to spear them. Makes about 4 dozen meatballs.

Teriyaki Sauce. Combine ⅓ cup soy sauce, 2 tablespoons *each* sugar and Sherry, ¾ teaspoons grated fresh ginger (or ¼ teaspoon ground ginger), and 2 cloves garlic (minced or mashed).

Pork Balls in Cheese Dip

Choose from two cheeses to flavor the smooth dip for these meatball appetizers. If you use Liederkranz, the sauce will have a robust flavor and bouquet; Camembert gives more subtle overtones. Use picks to spear and eat the meatballs.

    2 ounces Liederkranz or Camembert cheese,
       well chilled
    2 tablespoons butter or margarine
    ¼ cup coarsely chopped onion
    1 pound boneless fully-cooked ham, ground
    ½ pound boneless lean pork, ground
    ⅓ cup each milk and fine dry bread crumbs
    2 eggs
    2 tablespoons all-purpose flour
    ¾ cup water
    ½ cup dry white wine
    1 teaspoon chicken seasoned stock base or
       1 chicken bouillon cube

Using a paring knife, scrape and discard the thin outside crust from the cheese; set cheese aside.

In a small saucepan over medium-high heat, melt the butter; add the onion and sauté until golden (about 4 minutes). Remove from heat and, with a slotted spoon, transfer onions to a bowl; reserve butter in pan. Add to the onions the ham, pork, milk, bread crumbs, and eggs. Mix together with your hands until blended. Shape into 1-inch balls and set about 1 inch apart on greased, rimmed baking pans. Bake in a 500° oven, turning if needed to brown well on all sides (about 7 to 10 minutes). Spoon into a small serving bowl and keep warm while you make sauce.

Stir the flour into reserved butter; stir over medium-high heat until bubbly. Remove from heat and gradually stir in water and wine. Add chicken stock base and cook, stirring, until the mixture boils and thickens; remove from heat. Add cheese (cut in small pieces) and stir until it

melts. Pour into another serving bowl and keep warm with the meatballs. Makes about 6 dozen meatballs.

Appetizer Meatballs in Spicy Sauce

These bite-sized meatballs can be completely prepared a day ahead.

    ⅓ cup firmly packed brown sugar
    1 can (8 oz.) tomato sauce
    3 tablespoons lemon juice
    ⅛ teaspoon garlic salt
    ½ cup dry red wine (or ½ cup water plus
       1 tablespoon lemon juice)
    ⅓ cup shredded peeled potato (about
       1 small potato)
    1 pound lean ground beef
    1 small onion, finely minced
    1 egg
    ½ teaspoon salt

In a saucepan, combine the brown sugar, tomato sauce, lemon juice, garlic salt, and wine. Bring to a boil, stirring; reduce heat and allow to simmer gently, uncovered, until sauce is thickened (about 20 minutes).

Combine shredded potato, meat, onion, egg, and salt; shape into balls the size of large marbles.

Arrange on rimmed baking pans. Put into a 500° oven for 4 to 5 minutes or until lightly browned. Remove and add to the prepared sauce, including any pan juices. Cool, then cover and refrigerate if made ahead.

To serve, cover and heat meat and sauce together slowly. Makes about 5 dozen meatballs.

Appetizer Lamb Meatballs

Chopped mint gives a refreshing accent to these robustly seasoned ground lamb balls.

    2 pounds lean ground lamb
    2 teaspoons ground cumin seed
    2 teaspoons chopped fresh mint leaves or
       ½ teaspoon dried mint leaves
    2 green onions, finely chopped
    1½ teaspoons salt
    ¼ teaspoon pepper
    ¼ cup fine dry bread crumbs
    2 eggs
    1 cup sour cream
    1 teaspoon caraway seed

For meatballs, mix together the ground meat, cumin, mint, onions, salt, pepper, crumbs, and eggs. Shape into 1-inch balls. Place on greased, rimmed baking pans.

Bake in a 425° oven for 15 minutes or until well browned and no longer pink inside. Arrange meatballs on a platter or in a chafing dish with toothpicks alongside. Mix together the sour cream and caraway seed and serve in a bowl as a dipping sauce. Makes about 60 appetizers.

Four-Way Ground Beef Balls

Make the meatballs and any of the sauce recipes as much as a day ahead and refrigerate. To keep the meat tender and juicy, reheat slowly in the sauce just to the simmering point; add a small amount of additional broth to sauces, if needed. Regulate heat in a chafing dish or other tabletop heating device to keep meat and sauce warm for serving.

    2 *pounds lean ground beef*
    ½ *cup each fine dry bread crumbs and milk*
    2 *eggs*
 1½ *teaspoons salt (or part garlic salt)*
    1 *sauce recipe (choices follow)*

Combine meat, crumbs, milk, eggs, and salt in a bowl. Mix lightly to blend. Shape into balls about the size of large marbles. Arrange on shallow, rimmed baking pans. Bake in a 500° oven for 4 to 5 minutes or until lightly browned. Remove and add to the prepared sauce of your choice (sauce recipes follow); include any pan juices. Cool, then cover and refrigerate until time to serve. Reheat meat and sauce together, covered, over low heat, stirring gently several times; keep warm in chafing dish or over candle warmer. Makes about 100 meatballs.

Sweet and Sour Sauce

Drain syrup from 2 cans (about 13 oz. *each*) pineapple chunks; reserve pineapple. Combine pineapple syrup with 1¼ cups regular strength chicken broth, ¼ cup firmly packed brown sugar, ¾ cup vinegar, 1 tablespoon *each* soy sauce and catsup, and 4 tablespoons cornstarch. Cook over medium heat, stirring, until thickened. Add 1 cup thinly sliced green onions (including part of the tops) and 3 green peppers, seeded and cut in 1-inch squares. Cook 1 minute longer. Remove from heat and add pineapple chunks.

Curry Sauce

Heat ¼ cup (⅛ lb.) butter or margarine in a heavy pan over medium heat; add 1 large onion, (chopped) and sauté until limp. Stir in 1 clove garlic (mashed) and 2 tablespoons curry powder; cook about 1 minute more. Add 4 tablespoons all-purpose flour, 1 tablespoon cornstarch, 2 teaspoons sugar, ½ teaspoon salt, and dash cayenne; stir over medium heat until blended and bubbly. Gradually stir in 2 cups regular strength chicken broth and 1 cup whipping cream; cook until thickened.

Blue Cheese Sauce

Heat ¼ cup (⅛ lb.) butter or margarine in a pan over medium heat; stir in 4 tablespoons all-purpose flour and 1 clove garlic (minced or mashed) and cook until blended and bubbly. Gradually stir in 1 cup half-and-half (light cream) and 1½ cups regular strength chicken broth. Cook, stirring, until thickened. Crumble 4 oz. blue cheese, add to sauce, and stir until blended. Taste and add salt, if needed. Sprinkle with parsley just before serving.

Italian Tomato Sauce

Chop 4 slices bacon and sauté until crisp in a frying pan over medium heat. Drain and discard all but 2 tablespoons of the drippings. Add 1 medium-sized onion (chopped) to pan and cook until limp. Add 1 clove garlic (minced or mashed) and 1 can (1 lb. 12 oz.) pear-shaped tomatoes and their liquid (break up tomatoes with a fork),1 teaspoon *each* basil and oregano leaves, 1 bay leaf, and 1½ cups regular strength beef broth; simmer, uncovered, for about 20 minutes. Blend together 2 tablespoons cornstarch, ¼ cup dry red wine (or additional beef broth), 1 teaspoon sugar, ½ teaspoon salt, and ¼ teaspoon pepper. Stir into tomato mixture and cook until thickened. Stir in 1 cup grated Parmesan cheese; remove from heat.

Meat Loaf: 24 Variations

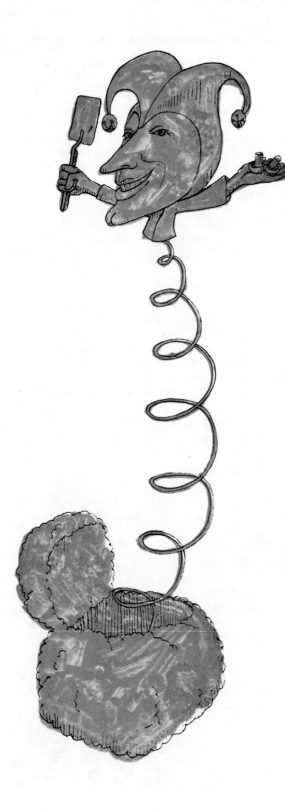

Meat Loaf with Vegetable Sauce

Bake this moist meat loaf in a decorative dish that you can bring to the table.

    2 pounds lean ground beef
    ¾ cup rolled oats (regular or quick-cooking)
    1½ teaspoons salt
    ¾ cup finely chopped onion
    6 tablespoons finely chopped parsley
    1 can (1 lb.) pear-shaped tomatoes
    2 tablespoons butter or margarine
    1 medium-sized carrot, chopped
    1 cup finely sliced celery
    ¼ cup chopped green pepper
    1 large can (15 oz.) tomato sauce

Combine beef, oats, salt, ½ cup of the onion, and 4 tablespoons of the parsley. Drain liquid from tomatoes into meat and mix well; set tomatoes aside. Pat the meat mixture into a loaf down the center of a shallow baking dish (about 9 by 13 inches). Bake, uncovered, in a 325° oven for 1 hour.

Meanwhile, melt butter in a frying pan over medium heat and sauté the remaining onion, carrot, celery, and green pepper for 10 minutes. Stir in tomato sauce, reserved tomatoes, and remaining parsley. Remove loaf from oven, skim fat from drippings, and pour sauce over loaf. Bake 15 minutes longer. Makes 6 to 8 servings.

Almond Studded Curry Loaf

Chutney and curry flavor this meat loaf; almonds bake on top.

    2 tablespoons butter or margarine
    1 small onion, finely chopped
    2 to 3 teaspoons curry powder
    ½ teaspoon salt
    1 tablespoon lemon juice
    1 tablespoon Major Grey's chutney, chopped
    ½ cup wheat germ or fine dry bread crumbs
    ½ cup milk
    1½ pounds lean ground beef
    1 egg
    ⅓ cup sliced almonds

In a frying pan, heat the butter over medium heat and sauté onion 3 minutes. Add curry and sauté 2 minutes. Remove from heat and add the salt, lemon juice, chutney, wheat germ, milk, beef, and egg. Mix until well blended. Lightly pat into a 9-inch pie pan. Sprinkle almonds over the top. Bake, uncovered, in a 375° oven for about 40 minutes. Makes 4 servings.

Cottage Cheese Meat Loaf

The small nuggets of cheese mixed with the beef make this meat loaf exceptionally moist and tender.

  1 *pound lean ground beef*
  1 *cup (½ pint) cottage cheese*
  1 *egg*
  ½ *cup quick-cooking rolled oats*
  ¼ *cup catsup*
  1 *tablespoon prepared mustard*
  2 *tablespoons chopped onion*
  ¾ *teaspoon salt*
  ⅛ *teaspoon pepper*
  ⅓ *cup grated Parmesan cheese*

Combine the ground beef with the cottage cheese, egg, rolled oats, catsup, prepared mustard, onion, salt, and pepper. Mix the ingredients lightly until well blended. Press the mixture loosely into a shallow baking pan (about 8 inches square). Bake, uncovered, in a 350° oven for 20 minutes. Remove from oven and sprinkle the Parmesan cheese evenly over the top. Return to the oven and continue to bake for 10 minutes longer. Let stand for about 5 minutes before cutting in squares to serve. Makes about 6 servings.

Beef Tartar with Caviar

Let guests help themselves to this attractive raw beef appetizer ringed with chopped white onion.

  ½ *pound lean ground beef*
  2 *to 4 tablespoons black caviar*
  ½ *to 1 cup finely chopped white onion*
    Sprigs of parsley for garnish
    Buffet-style rye bread

Shape the ground beef into an oval patty about ½ to ¾ inch thick. Put in the center of a serving plate. Score surface in a diamond pattern by pressing with edge of a knife, then top with 3 or 4 diagonally placed bands of the caviar. Surround the beef with chopped onion and garnish with sprigs of parsley. Spread on buffet-style rye bread. Makes 6 to 8 appetizer servings.

French Country-Style Meat Loaf

Here's a loaf that bakes in a 2-quart casserole. Let it cool, then chill thoroughly, so it is easy to slice for a hearty sandwich at home or on the road.

  1 *medium-sized onion, finely chopped*
  3 *tablespoons butter or margarine*
  ¼ *pound mushrooms, finely chopped*
  ¼ *cup brandy or Sherry*
  3 *eggs*
  ½ *cup condensed beef consommé, undiluted*
  4 *slices firm white bread, broken in small pieces*
  2 *cloves garlic*
  ½ *teaspoon each thyme leaves, ground allspice, and salt*
1½ *pounds lean ground beef*
  1 *pound lean ground pork*
  ½ *pound cooked ham, sliced ½ inch thick*
  ⅔ *cup pine nuts*

Using a large frying pan over medium heat, sauté onion in 2 tablespoons of the butter until limp; add mushrooms and remaining 1 tablespoon butter and sauté just until butter-coated (about 1 minute). Add brandy or Sherry and simmer 1 minute; let cool.

Place in a blender container the eggs, consommé, bread, garlic, thyme, allspice, and salt; blend until smooth. Turn beef and pork into a large bowl; mix in the sautéed vegetables and the egg mixture. Dice ham into ½-inch pieces. Add the ham and ⅓ cup of the pine nuts to the meat loaf mixture and mix well. Turn into a greased 2-quart casserole and sprinkle remaining nuts on top.

Bake, uncovered, in a 325° oven for 1½ hours or until well browned.

Let cool, cover, and chill. Remove any congealed fat from the side; slice ½ inch thick. Makes about 12 to 14 servings.

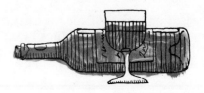

Grated Carrot Meat Loaf

A mustard-flavored sugary glaze bakes on this carrot-flecked ground beef loaf.

2 slices firm white bread, broken in pieces
¾ cup milk
2½ pounds lean ground beef
3 eggs
2 large carrots, finely shredded
2 tablespoons prepared horseradish
1 envelope (about 1½ oz.) onion soup mix
   (enough for 3 or 4 servings)
¼ cup catsup
3 tablespoons firmly packed brown sugar
2 tablespoons Dijon mustard

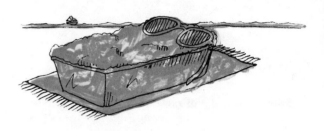

Whirl bread in a blender to make about 1½ cups fine crumbs. In a large mixing bowl, pour milk over bread crumbs and let stand until absorbed. Mix in ground beef, eggs, carrots, horseradish, and onion soup mix. Pat into a greased 5 by 9-inch loaf pan. For topping, mix together catsup, brown sugar, and mustard and spread evenly over the top. Bake, uncovered, in a 350° oven for 1½ hours. Makes 8 to 10 servings.

Family Meat Loaf

A spicy red glaze bakes on top of this well-seasoned beef mixture.

1½ pounds lean ground beef
⅔ cup quick-cooking rolled oats
1 cup milk
1 teaspoon salt
⅛ teaspoon pepper
¼ teaspoon poultry seasoning
2 eggs
1 teaspoon Worcestershire
1 small onion, finely chopped
¼ cup catsup
1½ to 2 tablespoons firmly packed brown sugar
1 teaspoon prepared mustard
⅛ teaspoon ground nutmeg

In a large mixing bowl, combine the ground beef, rolled oats, milk, salt, pepper, poultry seasoning, eggs, Worcestershire, and onion. Put in a loaf pan (about 5 by 9 inches). Set aside while you prepare the glaze.

In a measuring cup, combine the catsup, brown sugar, mustard, and nutmeg. Spread evenly over the meat loaf. Bake, uncovered, in a 350° oven for about 1 hour and 15 minutes. Makes 6 to 8 servings.

Super Meat Loaf

Shaped like a giant meatball, this spicy meat loaf is based on flavors reminiscent of Istanbul. It's made from ground lamb, seasoned with oregano and spices, and studded with pine nuts that toast with the loaf.

2 tablespoons butter or margarine
1 medium-sized onion, finely chopped
½ cup fine, dry bread crumbs
¼ cup dry red wine or tomato juice
1½ teaspoons salt
½ teaspoon oregano leaves, crumbled
¼ teaspoon each pepper, ground cinnamon, and nutmeg
⅓ cup finely chopped parsley
2 eggs
2 pounds lean ground lamb
⅓ cup pine nuts
   Parsley sprigs
   Lemon wedges
   About 1 carton (8 oz.) unflavored yogurt

In a frying pan, melt the butter over medium-high heat; add the onion and cook, stirring, until limp (about 5 minutes); turn into a large bowl. Add to the bowl the bread crumbs, wine, salt, oregano, pepper, cinnamon, nutmeg, chopped parsley, eggs, and ground lamb. Mix well.

Use your hands to form meat into a large, compact ball. Roll in pine nuts, pressing them into the meat. Set the meat loaf in a pie pan and bake, uncovered, in a 325° oven for 1 hour and 30 minutes or until nuts become golden. Transfer to a serving plate and garnish with parsley sprigs and lemon. To serve, cut in wedges and offer yogurt to spoon over the meat like a sauce. Makes about 6 servings.

Ham Loaf with Apple Rings

Apple rings and raisins crown this ham loaf. It's a good way to serve leftover ham for another meal.

      3 tablespoons butter or margarine
    ½ cup firmly packed brown sugar
  1½ cups apple juice or cider
      2 tart apples
    ½ cup seedless raisins
      3 cups ground cooked ham (about 1 lb.)
    ½ cup each fine soda cracker crumbs and finely
          chopped onion
      1 egg slightly beaten
      1 teaspoon prepared mustard
      2 tablespoons catsup

Combine butter, brown sugar, and 1 cup of the apple juice; boil, uncovered, 3 minutes. Peel and core the apples, then slice in about ½-inch-thick rings. Add apple slices and raisins to syrup; simmer, uncovered, 3 minutes; set aside. Combine the ham, crumbs, onion, egg, mustard, catsup, and remaining ½ cup apple juice; blend well. Turn into a shallow baking pan (about 9 by 13 inches) and shape into a compact loaf across center of pan. Lift apple rings from syrup and arrange, overlapping, across ends of pan on either side of the loaf. Spoon syrup and raisins over apples and ham loaf.

Bake, uncovered, in a 350° oven for about 45 minutes; baste several times with pan juices. Makes 6 servings.

Ham Loaf with Orange Sauce

Baste this loaf with spicy orange sauce as it bakes, then serve it with more of the sauce.

      About 1½ pounds cooked ham
      1 large carrot
      2 slices firm white bread
      2 eggs
      2 tablespoons minced onion
      1 teaspoon dry mustard
      1 can (6 oz.) frozen orange juice concentrate
      2 cups water
      2 tablespoons cornstarch
    ⅛ teaspoon each ground cinnamon and cloves
    ⅓ cup raisins (optional)

Using the fine blade of the food chopper, grind the ham (you should have 4 cups); then put the carrot and bread through the food chopper. In a bowl, combine the ham, carrot, bread, eggs, onion, and dry mustard. Combine orange juice concentrate with water; add ½ cup juice to ham; set aside remaining juice. Blend ham mixture well and shape into a 4 by 8-inch loaf in a shallow baking pan.

Blend cornstarch with reserved orange juice, cinnamon, and cloves; cook, stirring, until thickened. Add raisins (if used). Bake ham loaf, uncovered, in a 375° oven for about 35 minutes or until well glazed, basting several times with some of the orange sauce. Reheat remaining sauce and pass in a bowl at the table. Makes 4 to 6 servings.

Glazed Ham Loaf with Fruit Garnish

Apricots and prunes give a festive look and hint of sweetness to this meat loaf.

      Fruit Garnish (recipe follows)
  1½ pounds lean ground ham
    ¾ pound lean ground beef
    ¾ cup fine dry bread crumbs
      2 eggs
  1½ cups milk
    ½ teaspoon each dry mustard and ground cloves
    ¼ teaspoon salt

Prepare the fruit garnish; set aside. In a large bowl combine the ham, beef, bread crumbs, eggs, milk, mustard, cloves, and salt. Mix with your hands until well blended. Shape meat mixture into a loaf down the center of a 9 by 13-inch baking pan. Slowly pour about ⅓ cup of syrup (drained from Fruit Garnish) evenly over the top. Bake, uncovered, in a 350° oven about 1 hour 15 minutes or until richly glazed, basting several times with more of the fruit syrup. About 10 minutes before the loaf is done, pour remaining syrup over loaf and arrange fruit in the pan along the sides of the loaf to heat.

Lift loaf from pan onto a serving platter; surround with fruit. Makes 8 servings.

Fruit Garnish. In a pan combine 1 cup each dried apricots and pitted prunes, 2 cups water, ¼ teaspoon grated lemon peel, and ½ cup sugar. Simmer, uncovered, for 15 minutes.

Turkey Loaf

You bake this meat loaf well in advance, then slice and serve it cold like a French terrine.

- 1 large onion, chopped
- 2 tablespoons butter or margarine
- 2 pounds ground turkey
- ½ cup whipping cream
- 2 eggs
- 1 teaspoon salt
- ¼ teaspoon pepper
- ⅔ cup fine dry bread crumbs
- ½ teaspoon ground nutmeg
- About ½ pound Polish sausage

In a frying pan over medium heat sauté the onion in the butter until soft; set aside. In a large bowl mix together the ground turkey, whipping cream, eggs, salt, pepper, bread crumbs, nutmeg, and the onion. Spoon half of the meat mixture in an even layer in a 1½-quart deep oval or round casserole. Arrange Polish sausage on meat layer. (If casserole is round, mark direction that the sausages point.) Cover sausage with remaining meat mixture, patting it smoothly and compactly into casserole. Cover and set inside a larger pan with about 1½ inches hot water.

Bake in a 350° oven for 2 hours. Lift casserole from hot water and let cool to room temperature. Then refrigerate (still covered) until thoroughly chilled, at least 6 hours or overnight. Pour off juices and spoon over top of loaf. Cut in thin vertical slices at right angles to the direction the sausages point in dish. Makes 6 to 8 servings.

Little Lamb Loaves

Make these meat loaves in muffin pans and they'll bake in just 15 minutes.

- 1 pound lean ground lamb
- ½ pound lean ground beef
- 2 cups soft French bread crumbs
- 1 can (10½ oz.) condensed onion soup
- ¼ teaspoon oregano leaves
- Mint leaves

Mix ground lamb, beef, crumbs, soup, and oregano, stirring just until blended. Spoon meat mixture into 12 ungreased 2½-inch muffin cups, pressing in lightly. Bake, uncovered, in a 400° oven for about 15 minutes or until well browned and no longer pink inside. Garnish with fresh mint leaves. Makes 6 servings of 2 loaves each.

Mushroom Veal Loaf

A sour cream-caper sauce and crisp bacon flavor this veal and ham loaf.

- ⅓ pound mushrooms, chopped
- 1 small onion, chopped
- 3 tablespoons butter or margarine
- 2 pounds ground veal
- ½ pound ground ham
- 3 eggs
- ¾ cup crushed saltine crackers
- ½ cup milk
- ¼ cup prepared horseradish
- 3 tablespoons chile sauce
- ½ teaspoon salt
- ¼ teaspoon garlic salt
- ¼ cup finely chopped parsley
- 3 slices bacon, cut in half crosswise
- 1 tablespoon each cornstarch and cold water
- ½ cup sour cream
- 1 tablespoon capers, drained

Sauté chopped mushrooms and onion in butter over medium heat for five minutes; set aside. Mix veal, ham, eggs, cracker crumbs, milk, horseradish, chile sauce, salt, garlic salt, parsley, and the sautéed vegetables. Pat mixture into a greased 5 by 9-inch loaf pan. Partially cook the bacon to render out most of the fat (bacon should still be limp and not browned); drain and arrange over meat.

Bake, uncovered, in a 350° oven for 1½ hours. Lift loaf to a serving platter; keep warm. Discard fat from pan drippings and stir in cornstarch blended with cold water and sour cream; cook, stirring until sauce is thickened. Add capers and pass hot sauce to spoon over slices of meat loaf. Makes about 8 servings.

Pizza-Topped Meat Loaf

A Neapolitan inspiration: this entrée bakes quickly in a shallow pan. Cut in squares and serve on toasted French bread slices.

2 pounds lean ground beef
½ cup each milk and saltine cracker crumbs
2 eggs, slightly beaten
½ cup finely chopped onions
½ teaspoon each salt, garlic salt, oregano leaves, and basil leaves
1 can (10½ oz.) pizza sauce
  Extra toppings (suggestions follow)
1 cup shredded Mozzarella cheese (about 4 oz.)
½ cup grated Parmesan cheese
  French bread, sliced and toasted

In a bowl combine the ground beef, milk, cracker crumbs, eggs, onion, salt, garlic salt, oregano, and basil. Mix until well blended, then lightly pat into a 9 by 13-inch baking pan. Bake, uncovered, in a 400° oven for 20 minutes. Remove from oven, drain off excess drippings, and spread pizza sauce over top. Distribute any of the extra toppings you choose over meat, then sprinkle evenly with the Mozzarella and Parmesan cheeses. Put back into the oven, uncovered, for about 10 minutes until cheese is bubbly. Cut in squares and serve at once on toasted French bread slices. Makes 6 to 8 servings.

Extra toppings. Use any one of these toppings or some of each: ¾ cup sliced pitted ripe olives; ½ seeded green pepper, cut in strips; or 1 cup sliced raw mushrooms.

Bobotie

Bobotie (bah-boo-tee) comes from South Africa. It's a meat loaf spiced with curry and laced with fruit and nuts. Serve with rice and chutney.

2 medium-sized onions, chopped
1 tart apple, peeled and diced
2 tablespoons butter or margarine
3 teaspoons curry powder
2 pounds lean ground beef
½ cup fine dry bread crumbs
2 eggs
1½ cups milk
2 tablespoons vinegar
2 tablespoons apricot jam or sugar
1½ teaspoons salt
¼ teaspoon pepper
½ cup sliced almonds, toasted
6 whole bay leaves

In a frying pan, sauté the onion and apple in butter over medium heat until soft (about 10 minutes). Stir in curry, cook about 1 minute, then turn into a bowl. Add the ground beef, bread crumbs, 1 of the eggs, ½ cup of the milk, the vinegar, apricot jam, salt, pepper, and almonds. Use your hands to mix the ingredients well, then pack into a shallow baking dish (about 8 by 12 inches or 9 by 13 inches). Arrange bay leaves on top and bake, uncovered, in a 350° oven for about 50 minutes.

Lightly beat together the remaining egg and 1 cup milk. Remove dish from oven and skim off fat; slowly pour egg mixture over top. Return to oven for 10 minutes. Makes 6 servings.

Meat Loaves with a Surprise Inside

Beef Bacon Rolls

Individual rolls are stuffed and wrapped with bacon.

8 slices bacon
  About ½ slice firm white bread
1 tablespoon minced parsley
1 pound lean ground beef
1 teaspoon instant minced onion
½ teaspoon each seasoned pepper and salt

Fry 4 slices of the bacon until crisp; lift out bacon, drain, crumble, and set aside. Discard all but 2 tablespoons of the drippings. Whirl bread in a blender to make ¼ cup fine crumbs. Brown bread crumbs in the 2 tablespoons drippings. Remove from heat; stir in parsley and crumbled bacon; reserve. Season ground beef with instant minced onion, seasoned pepper, and salt.

On a board, pat meat mixture out to form a 10-inch square; quarter to get 4 smaller squares. Place a line of bacon-crumb filling down the center of each square; bring together the meat edges that run parallel to the filling and gently shape into a roll. Wrap a strip of uncooked bacon around each meat roll and fasten with a toothpick. Arrange rolls on the rack of a broiler pan. Bake, uncovered, in a 400° oven for about 15 minutes or until bacon is crisp and meat is still slightly pink inside. Makes 4 servings.

Meat Loaf in a Terrine

You can easily transport this cold meat loaf to a picnic site for hearty outdoor sandwiches.

About 1 pound sliced bacon
3 or 4 chicken livers
3 tablespoons butter or margarine
2 small onions, finely chopped
1½ pounds ground pork loin end or lean ground beef
2 eggs
1 teaspoon salt
¾ cup all-purpose flour
1 cup milk
½ to ¾ pound cooked sausages (directions follow)
2 bay leaves
A few whole black peppers
Sliced French bread (optional)

Use bacon slices to line the bottom and sides of an 8 to 9-cup, deep, straight-sided casserole or loaf pan; the bacon slices should just meet in pan bottom, with ends draped over the rim.

In a frying pan cook the chicken livers in butter for 2 to 3 minutes over medium heat, just to firm but not to cook them; turn once. Remove livers and add onion to pan; cook, stirring, until soft.

Next, beat thoroughly in an electric mixer (or vigorously by hand) the ground pork or beef, eggs, salt, and flour; blend in milk and onions with butter.

Spoon enough meat mixture into bacon-lined casserole to make an even ½-inch-thick layer; top with chicken livers. Cover livers with a smooth layer of a little more meat. Lay the cooked sausages parallel and slightly apart on meat and cover with remainder of the meat; smooth top. Fold bacon over meat; lay bay leaves and peppers on bacon. Cover and bake in a 375° oven 1 hour and 15 minutes.

Remove from heat, cool briefly, then chill thoroughly (overnight if possible). To serve, slice meat loaf vertically in casserole and lift out slices; if desired, scrape off fat. Serve meat on a plate or on sliced French bread. Makes 6 to 8 servings.

Cooked sausages. Use links or loops of highly seasoned sausages such as linguisa, Italian fresh garlic sausages, or Polish sausages. Put sausages in a saucepan, cover with water, bring to a boil, and simmer for 20 minutes. Drain well and use hot or cold.

Italian Veal Loaf

Garlic-flavored sausages pierce the center of this chilled Italian veal and beef loaf.

About 12 ounces mild Italian pork sausages
Water
3 eggs
⅓ cup dry white wine or regular strength chicken broth
⅓ cup sour cream
5 slices firm white bread, broken into pieces
1½ teaspoons salt
2 cloves garlic
¼ teaspoon ground nutmeg
½ small onion, chopped
⅛ teaspoon pepper
1 pound lean ground beef
1½ pounds ground veal
6 pickled whole sweet red cherry peppers for garnish

Place the sausages in a saucepan, cover with water, and simmer, covered, for 20 minutes; drain and cool. In a blender container place the eggs, wine, sour cream, bread, salt, garlic, nutmeg, onion, and pepper; blend until smooth. Place the ground beef and veal in a bowl; add the egg mixture, mixing until blended.

Line up the sausages lengthwise on a greased baking pan at least 14 inches long. Pat meat mixture over, around, and under the sausages, to encase them and make a log 4 inches wide and 14 inches long. Bake, uncovered, in a 375° oven for 45 minutes or until loaf is no longer pink in the center when pierced with a sharp knife. Let cool, cover, and chill.

To serve, place meat loaf on a board and garnish top with the sweet peppers. Cut loaf in ½-inch thick slices. Makes about 10 to 12 servings.

Stuffed Meat Loaf

The bread stuffing in the center of this rolled loaf absorbs flavor from the cooking meat.

1½ pounds lean ground beef
¾ pound lean ground pork
1½ teaspoons salt
¼ teaspoon pepper
 1 egg
½ cup seedless raisins
 4 cups toasted bread cubes
⅓ cup minced onion
 2 tablespoons minced parsley
¼ teaspoon each ground sage and pepper
¼ teaspoon salt
⅔ cup hot, regular strength beef broth or water

Mix beef, pork, the 1½ teaspoons salt, ¼ teaspoon pepper, and egg. On a sheet of waxed paper, pat out meat mixture evenly to form a square about ½ inch thick. Mix raisins, bread, onion, parsley, sage, pepper, ¼ teaspoon salt, and broth. Pat in an even layer over the meat. Roll as for a jelly roll and place in a baking pan seam side down. Bake, uncovered, in a 350° oven about 1 hour and 15 minutes. Serve sliced, hot or cold. Makes 8 servings.

Caraway Rye Meat Loaf

A few slices of caraway rye bread give distinctive flavor to this moist meat loaf.

 5 thin slices caraway rye bread
½ cup each milk and tomato juice
 2 eggs
 2 pounds lean ground beef
 1 medium-sized onion, finely chopped
1½ teaspoons salt
¼ teaspoon pepper
¼ teaspoon ground nutmeg or mace
½ teaspoon each marjoram and savory leaves

Crumble the bread slices into a large bowl (makes about 3 cups); add the milk and tomato juice, then let mixture stand about 15 minutes, stirring several times. Add eggs to the bread mixture and beat with a fork until well blended. Add the meat, onion, salt, pepper, nutmeg or mace, marjoram, and savory. Use your hands or a spoon to mix the ingredients together. Pat into a 9 by 5-inch loaf pan. Bake, uncovered, in a 350° oven for about 1 hour and 15 minutes. Lift out of pan and slice to serve. Makes about 8 servings.

Mushroom-Stuffed Meat Loaf

Packed with treats, the meat loaf encases a savory mushroom and onion stuffing for this good looking, inexpensive, company entrée.

½ pound medium-sized mushrooms, sliced
 1 large onion, chopped
½ cup finely sliced celery
 2 tablespoons butter or margarine
¾ cup tomato juice
1½ slices firm white bread
1½ teaspoons salt
⅛ teaspoon pepper
 2 pounds lean ground beef
 2 eggs

In a frying pan over medium heat, sauté mushrooms, onion, and celery in butter until vegetables are limp. Add ½ cup of the tomato juice, and simmer for 10 minutes. Break the bread into small pieces and whirl in a blender to make about 1 cup fine crumbs. Mix crumbs, ½ teaspoon of the salt, and the pepper into the vegetable mixture; set aside. Mix ground beef with remaining 1 teaspoon salt, remaining ¼ cup tomato juice, and eggs. Shape meat mixture into a loaf down the center of a greased baking pan (about 9 by 13 inches). With a spoon, scoop out a layer of meat from the center of the loaf to make a lengthwise cavity; evenly distribute the mushroom mixture in the cavity and pat the scooped out meat over the stuffing to completely enclose it with meat. Bake, uncovered, in a 350° oven 1 hour and 15 minutes or until well browned. Makes about 8 servings.

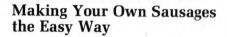

Making Your Own Sausages the Easy Way

Using clear roasting film that comes in 18-inch rolls, is an easy way to shape homemade sausages. You can make your own sausages without bothering to search for, and then prepare, the fresh casings.

Start with meats ground by your meatman for either of the following sausages. The first is a robustly seasoned mixture of beef and pork. The second, a combination of veal and pork, is milder; it tastes something like bockwurst.

These sausages are shaped as you wrap them in the roasting film. As an extra convenience, you cook the sausages in the oven, still in their roasting-film wrappers, and they turn out juicy and browned.

Once you've wrapped and shaped the sausages, you can keep them for a day or so in your refrigerator or freeze them for as long as two weeks—then thaw and bake.

To shape sausages (about 6 inches long and 1 inch thick) tear from an 18-inch-wide roll of clear roasting film four pieces that are each 8 inches long; place on a flat surface. Divide one recipe's worth of sausage mixture (recipes follow) in four equal portions. Spoon one portion of the sausage in a 14-inch-long band onto each piece of the roasting film, distributing evenly along one long side.

Roll meat up tightly in the film, smoothing it with your hands as you go to make an even, compact roll. Counter-twist ends, turning one in the direction opposite of the other, until a firm roll is formed; tie ends with string to close securely. Repeat to make three more rolls. Tie each sausage roll with string in the center to form two big sausages.

To bake sausages, place wrapped sausages in a single layer, slightly apart, on a rack in a rimmed baking pan. With a sharp, pointed knife prick small holes through the film at 1-inch intervals on top halves of the sausages. Bake in a 325° oven until well browned about 1 hour and 10 minutes. (For refrigerated or thawed frozen sausages allow 1 hour and 20 minutes.)

Beef and Pork Sausage

1 tablespoon butter or margarine
½ cup finely chopped green onion, including part of the tops
1 clove garlic, minced or mashed
½ teaspoon each rosemary and thyme leaves, crushed
¼ teaspoon ground cloves
1 pound each lean ground beef and lightly seasoned bulk pork sausage
1 teaspoon each salt and sugar
½ teaspoon pepper
¼ cup each all-purpose flour and nonfat dry milk
½ cup water

Melt butter in a small frying pan over medium-high heat. Add onion, garlic, rosemary, thyme, and cloves; sauté for 5 minutes or until onion is soft. Combine the onion mixture with the beef, sausage, salt, sugar, pepper, flour, nonfat dry milk, and water and mix well. Wrap and shape as directed. Makes 8 sausages.

Veal and Pork Sausage

1 tablespoon butter or margarine
¼ cup each finely chopped parsley and green onion, including part of tops
¼ teaspoon each rubbed sage, ground cloves, and mace or nutmeg
1 pound each ground veal and lightly seasoned bulk pork sausage
1 teaspoon each salt and sugar
¼ teaspoon pepper
¼ cup each all-purpose flour and nonfat dry milk
½ cup water
2 eggs, slightly beaten

Melt butter in a small frying pan over medium-high heat. Put in the parsley, onion, sage, cloves, and mace and sauté for 5 minutes or until onion is soft. Combine the onion mixture with the veal, sausage, salt, sugar, pepper, flour, nonfat dry milk, water, and eggs and mix thoroughly. Wrap and shape as directed. Makes 8 sausages.

Ham Loaf in Sour Cream Crust

Particularly adaptable to entertaining is this handsome ground ham loaf, baked in a decorative crust. It can be served hot or cold at a party buffet or picnic. Most preparation can be completed well in advance.

    2 pounds (about 4 cups lightly packed) lean
        ground cooked ham
    2 tablespoons minced onion
    ½ cup shredded Swiss cheese
    1 egg, slightly beaten
    1 can (3 or 4 oz.) chopped mushrooms
        Sour Cream Crust Dough (directions follow)
        Milk
        Sour cream

Combine the ground ham, minced onion, Swiss cheese, egg, and mushrooms with their liquid and stir to blend well; cover and keep cool until ready to use.

Cut the Sour Cream Crust Dough in half and roll out one section on a floured board to make a rectangle 6 by 14 inches; trim edges even and save scraps. Place dough rectangle on an ungreased baking sheet; roll out the other half of the dough on the floured board to make a second 6 by 14-inch rectangle. Trim edges and save scraps.

Distribute ham mixture lengthwise down the center of the dough on the baking sheet and, with your hands, firmly press the meat into a loaf about 3 inches in diameter, leaving a 1½-inch margin of dough on all sides.

Fold dough up against sides of the meat and brush outside edge lightly with milk. Fit second piece of dough over the loaf and press side securely against the sides of the bottom section of dough to seal. Prick the loaf in several places with a fork. At this point you can wrap loaf tightly and refrigerate as long as overnight.

Brush covering dough with milk. Roll reserved dough scraps out together on a floured board, cut into decorative shapes, and arrange them on the loaf. Bake loaf, uncovered, in a 375° oven 30 to 35 minutes or until crust is golden brown.

Serve hot or cold, cut in thick slices. Pass additional sour cream to spoon over individual portions. Makes 6 to 8 servings.

Sour Cream Crust Dough. In a bowl, mix 2 cups unsifted all-purpose flour with ½ teaspoon salt, then finely cut in ¾ cup (⅜ lb.) butter or margarine (or crumble with your fingers). Beat 1 egg with ½ cup sour cream and stir into flour mixture until it holds together. With your hands, press dough into a ball. Keep covered in a cool place or refrigerate until ready to use.

Strudel Meat Roll

Viennese strudels with crisp paper-thin outer-wraps are fine make-ahead party entrées. We streamline the procedure by substituting commercial fila dough (available in some gourmet shops and Near Eastern food markets) for the usual pulled strudel dough.

    1 small onion, finely chopped
    4 tablespoons butter or margarine
    ¼ pound mushrooms, chopped
    2 pounds lean ground beef
    1½ teaspoons salt
    ¼ teaspoon pepper
    ½ teaspoon oregano leaves, crumbled
    2 cloves garlic, minced
    3 eggs
    1½ cups shredded Swiss cheese
    ¼ cup finely chopped parsley
    ¼ cup fine dry bread crumbs
    12 sheets fila dough (each about 12 by 18 inches)
        Sour cream

In a large frying pan over medium heat, sauté onion in 2 tablespoons of the butter until transparent. Add mushrooms and meat and sauté until meat loses its pinkness, stirring until crumbly. Turn into a large bowl and season with salt, pepper, oregano, and garlic; let cool slightly. Add eggs and mix lightly. Then mix in the cheese, parsley, and crumbs. Chill.

Take 6 sheets of fila (keep remainder covered with clear plastic film) and overlap them to make a 15 by 24-inch rectangle (arrange layers to distribute as evenly as possible). Melt the remaining butter and use to brush fila lightly as you go so layers stick together.

Spread cooled filling over fila to within 1½ inches of the long sides and 3 inches of each end. Fold the 1½-inch edges over the filling. Then fold one of the 3-inch edges of fila over meat and continue rolling up like a compact jelly roll. Lay out 6 more sheets of fila to make a 15 by 24-inch rectangle, brush with butter, and fold in long sides 1½ inches. Set meat roll across a narrow end and roll up. Brush with remaining butter and place on a 10 by 15-inch baking pan.

Bake, uncovered, in a 375° oven for 30 to 35 minutes or until roll is golden brown. (If made ahead, chill covered; reheat in a 375° oven for 30 minutes.) Transfer to a serving platter and serve at table, cut in 1-inch slices. Pass sour cream to spoon over slices. Makes 6 servings of 2 slices.

A Mixed Bag of Oven Dishes

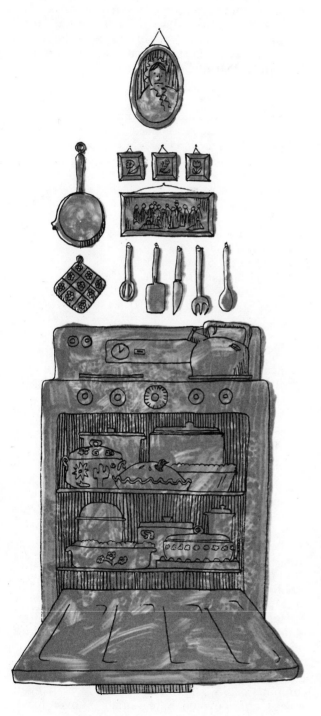

Artichoke Moussaka

Traditionally eggplant slices are layered with a zesty lamb filling in moussaka (moo-*sah*-ka), a classic dish of the Near East. Here frozen artichokes replace the eggplant, making the dish easier to prepare.

  2 tablespoons butter or margarine
  1 medium-sized onion, chopped
  2 pounds lean ground lamb
  ½ cup dry red wine or tomato juice
  2 medium-sized tomatoes, peeled and
       coarsely chopped
  ⅔ cup finely chopped parsley
  ¼ teaspoon each pepper, ground cinnamon, and
       ground nutmeg
1½ teaspoons salt
     Egg Sauce (recipe follows)
  1 bag (10 oz.) frozen artichoke bottoms (crowns),
       or 1 package (8 oz.) frozen artichoke hearts
  1 cup freshly shredded Parmesan cheese

In a large frying pan, melt the butter over medium-high heat; add the onion and lamb, breaking meat apart with a spoon until meat loses its pinkness. Add wine, tomatoes, parsley, pepper, cinnamon, nutmeg, and salt.

Simmer, uncovered, stirring occasionally for about 35 minutes or until liquid evaporates. Remove from heat, skim off any extra fat, and stir in 3 tablespoons of the Egg Sauce.

Spread the mixture in a greased 9 by 13-inch baking pan. Pour artichoke bottoms or hearts into a colander and run hot water over them until thawed; drain. (Cut hearts in quarters.) Press artichokes into meat. Spread remaining Egg Sauce over artichokes and sprinkle cheese on top. (At this point, it can be covered and chilled.)

Bake, uncovered, in a 350° oven for 20 minutes or until heated through (about 50 minutes if refrigerated). Remove from oven and let stand for about 10 minutes. Cut in squares to serve. Makes 12 servings.

Egg Sauce. In a bowl beat 3 eggs, ⅛ teaspoon ground nutmeg, and 1 teaspoon salt; set aside. In a saucepan melt ¼ cup (⅛ lb.) butter over medium heat. Add ¼ cup flour and cook, stirring, until bubbly. Remove from heat and gradually stir in 3 cups milk; cook, stirring, until it boils and thickens. Gradually stir about ⅓ of the hot sauce into the eggs. Then stir egg mixture back into hot sauce; cook about 1 minute. Remove from heat.

Pastitsio

Consider this Greek casserole you can assemble ahead for a buffet dinner party.

> 2 medium-sized onions, chopped
> ¼ cup (⅛ lb.) butter or margarine
> 2 pounds lean ground beef
>   Dash each ground cinnamon, cloves, and allspice
> 2 teaspoons salt
> ½ teaspoon pepper
> ½ cup water
> 2 tablespoons tomato paste
> 1 package (1 lb.) elbow macaroni
> 3 eggs, slightly beaten
>   Cream Sauce (recipe follows)
> ¾ cup grated Parmesan cheese

In a frying pan over medium heat, sauté onion in butter until golden. Add meat and cook, stirring, until well browned. Add cinnamon, cloves, allspice, 1½ teaspoons of the salt, and pepper. Stir in water and tomato paste; simmer, uncovered, for 5 minutes. Set aside.

Cook macaroni according to directions on package. Drain and mix with the eggs and remaining ½ teaspoon salt. Set aside while making Cream Sauce.

Spoon half of the macaroni mixture into a buttered 9 by 13-inch baking pan and sprinkle with ¼ cup of the Parmesan cheese. Place all of the meat mixture on top. Pour remaining macaroni mixture over meat and sprinkle with another ¼ cup of the Parmesan cheese. Then pour all the Cream Sauce over the macaroni; sprinkle top with remaining ¼ cup Parmesan cheese. (This much can be done ahead; cover and refrigerate as long as overnight.) Bake, uncovered, in a 350° oven for 45 minutes or until thoroughly heated (if refrigerated, bake for 1 hour). Makes 10 servings.

Cream Sauce. Melt 6 tablespoons butter in a saucepan over medium heat. Stir in ¾ cup all-purpose flour and cook, stirring, until blended and bubbly. Gradually stir in 1 quart milk and 1 teaspoon salt; cook, stirring, until sauce is bubbly and thickened. Remove from heat and very gradually pour sauce into 3 slightly beaten eggs until well blended.

Bohemian-Style Cabbage Rolls

Beef-stuffed cabbage rolls, baked in a red tomato sauce enriched by the meat juices during cooking, make a pleasant, convenient entrée. You can make it ahead or freeze it for another day.

> 1 pound lean ground beef
> 1 egg
> 1 teaspoon salt
> ½ teaspoon caraway seed
> ¼ teaspoon pepper
> ¼ cup fine dry bread crumbs
> 1 large onion
> 12 large whole cabbage leaves
>   Boiling salted water
>   Tomato Sauce (recipe follows)

In a bowl combine the ground beef, egg, salt, caraway seed, pepper, and fine dry bread crumbs. Cut onion in half; cut 1 portion in thin slices and set aside; finely chop remaining onion and add to meat mixture. Mix until blended.

Divide meat mixture into 12 equal portions. Shape each portion into an oblong about 2½ inches long and 1 inch thick.

Plunge cabbage leaves into boiling salted water and let cook until limp (about 5 minutes). Lift leaves from water and drain. Cut thick stem end from each leaf and reserve for sauce. Place 1 portion meat on each cabbage leaf near the stem end and roll to enclose meat. Tuck ends under and place rolls seam side down in a 2-quart shallow baking dish. Pour tomato sauce over cabbage rolls. Cover tightly with foil. Refrigerate if made ahead (or freeze).

Bake cabbage rolls, covered, in a 375° oven for 30 minutes (about 40 minutes if refrigerated) or until cabbage is very tender. (If frozen, bake unthawed rolls, covered, for 1 hour.) Let stand 10 minutes before serving to allow meat to reabsorb some of the juice. Makes 4 to 6 servings.

Tomato Sauce. Pour 1 large can (1 lb. 12 oz.) pear-shaped tomatoes (including the liquid) into a wide frying pan; mash tomatoes with a wooden spoon. Finely chop reserved cabbage stems and add to tomatoes with remaining sliced onion, 3 tablespoons *each* firmly packed brown sugar and vinegar, ¼ cup catsup, and ¼ teaspoon *each* rosemary and oregano leaves, crushed. Bring to boiling; then reduce heat, and simmer, uncovered, stirring occasionally until liquid is reduced to 2 cups.

Lamb-Stuffed Cabbage Leaves

Savory ground lamb and rice fill these cabbage leaves that you serve with a sour cream sauce.

    1 large head (about 2 lbs.) cabbage
    4 quarts boiling salted water
    1 pound lean ground lamb
    1 medium-sized onion, chopped
 1½ cups cooked rice
    4 tablespoons melted butter or margarine
    ½ cup fine dry bread crumbs
    ¾ teaspoon salt
    ¼ teaspoon each pepper, rubbed sage, oregano
        leaves, and rosemary leaves
      Sour Cream Sauce (recipe follows)

Cut out core from head of cabbage and discard outer leaves. Holding cabbage under running cold water, carefully remove leaves one at a time, letting the water help you separate them without tearing. You will need about 12 to 14 leaves, depending on size (save small inside leaves for salad). Cook 3 or 4 cabbage leaves at a time in the boiling water; cook just until bright green and limp (about 3 minutes). Remove leaves from water with tongs and allow to drain and cool.

For the filling, combine in a large bowl the meat, chopped onion, cooked rice, melted butter, bread crumbs, salt, pepper, sage, oregano, and rosemary; mix until ingredients are thoroughly blended.

To fill cabbage leaves, use 3 to 4 tablespoons of the meat mixture on the largest leaves; use 2 to 3 tablespoons for the smaller leaves. Spoon the meat near the base of each leaf. With the base of the leaf nearest you, fold the leaf base up over the meat, then roll toward the tip of the leaf. Hold the roll with the seam underneath and fold the outer edges of the leaf under, making a pillow-shaped roll.

Place the cabbage rolls in rows in a 9 by 13-inch greased baking pan; cover tightly with foil. (This much can be done ahead; then refrigerate.) Bake, covered, in a 350° oven for 30 minutes (45 minutes if refrigerated) or until heated through. Serve with Sour Cream Sauce. Makes 4 to 6 servings.

Sour Cream Sauce. Combine 2 tablespoons paprika with 2 cups sour cream; mix until well blended, then cover and refrigerate to chill and blend flavors. Serve cold or at room temperature.

Beef-Stuffed Pepper Halves

Mexican seasonings and tortilla chips flavor the ground beef filling. Use red bell peppers, for they retain their bright color and sweetness when baked.

    4 large red bell peppers
    1 teaspoon salt
    1 pound lean ground beef
    1 medium-sized onion, chopped
    2 cloves garlic, minced or mashed
    ½ teaspoon each ground cumin seed and
        oregano leaves
    1 tablespoon chile powder
 1½ cups tortilla or corn chips
    1 can (2¼ oz.) sliced ripe olives, drained
    1 can (8 oz.) tomato sauce
    ⅓ cup grated Parmesan cheese
    1 cup water

Cut the peppers in half lengthwise; discard seeds and stems. Arrange, cut side up, in a shallow casserole or baking pan about 9 by 13 inches.

Sprinkle salt in a frying pan; place over medium heat. Add the beef, onion, garlic, cumin, oregano, and chile powder. Cook, stirring frequently, until meat is crumbly (about 5 minutes). Break chips into small pieces and mix into the meat with the olives. Spoon mixture evenly into pepper shells, then pour tomato sauce evenly over top and sprinkle each with cheese. Pour water around peppers and bake, uncovered, in a 350° oven for 30 minutes or until peppers are tender when pierced. Makes 4 to 8 servings.

Baked Brunch Eggs

A fresh tomato half resting in a meaty sauce holds each egg while it bakes.

  3 medium-sized tomatoes
  3 tablespoons butter or margarine
  1 small onion, sliced
  ½ cup diced green pepper
  ½ clove garlic, mashed
  ½ pound lean ground beef
  ¼ pound lean bulk pork sausage
  2 tablespoons all-purpose flour
  ½ teaspoon each salt and chile powder
    Dash pepper
  6 eggs
  ¼ pound jack cheese

Peel and halve tomatoes and scoop out centers, discarding seeds and reserving pulp; set aside. In a frying pan, melt butter over medium heat; add onion, green pepper, and garlic and sauté until vegetables are limp. Add ground beef, pork sausage, and tomato pulp; cook, uncovered, over medium heat, stirring often for 10 minutes.

Combine flour, salt, chile powder, and pepper and sprinkle over the meat mixture; mix in well. Cook 3 or 4 minutes longer or until thickened. Turn mixture into an 8 by 12-inch baking pan. Arrange tomato shells, rounded side down, on the meat mixture. Carefully crack each egg and place one in each tomato shell. Cut cheese into 12 strips and cross two strips over each egg-filled tomato. Bake, uncovered, in a 350° oven for 20 to 25 minutes (remove from oven when whites are set but yolks are still runny). Makes 6 servings.

Ground Beef and Cheese Pie

A creamy layer of cottage cheese custard bakes on top of this ground beef pie.

    Quick Pastry (recipe follows)
  ½ teaspoon salt
  1½ pounds lean ground beef
  1 medium-sized onion, chopped
  ¼ teaspoon pepper
  1 whole egg
  1 egg white
  1 pint large curd cottage cheese
  ⅓ cup shredded Parmesan cheese
    Chopped parsley (optional)

Roll out the pastry on a lightly floured board to fit into a 9-inch pie pan; make a fluted edge.

Sprinkle salt in a frying pan, add meat, and cook over medium heat, stirring until juices begin to form. Then add onion and pepper and cook, stirring, until the meat loses all pinkness and liquid has evaporated. Turn into the prepared crust. In a bowl mix together the egg, egg white, and cottage cheese; spoon over the meat in the pie. Sprinkle top with Parmesan. Bake, uncovered, in a 375° oven for about 25 minutes or until top is set. Serve hot, sprinkled with parsley, if desired. Makes about 6 servings.

Quick Pastry. Combine in a bowl 1 cup biscuit mix, 1 egg yolk, and 2½ tablespoons milk. Mix with a fork until blended, then press into a ball.

Beef and Sausage Turnovers

Spicy, nut-studded meat filling is encased in triangles of sour cream pastry. If you make them ahead, loosely enclose in foil to reheat.

    Sour Cream Pastry (recipe follows)
  2 mild Italian pork sausages (about 6 oz.)
  ½ pound lean ground beef
  ¼ cup pine nuts (optional)
  2 green onions, sliced
  2 eggs
  2 tablespoons sour cream
    Salt and pepper to taste

Prepare pastry; chill at least 1 hour. For the filling, remove casings from sausage, crumble, and sauté in a frying pan over medium heat with beef and nuts (if used) until browned. Remove from heat, mix in onions, 1 egg, and sour cream; season with salt and pepper.

Roll out pastry on a floured board into a 10 by 20-inch rectangle; cut into 8 squares. Fill each with ⅛ of the filling. Dampen edges, fold over into triangles, press edges to seal, prick tops, and brush with remaining egg, beaten. Bake on an ungreased baking sheet in a 400° oven for 20 to 25 minutes until browned. Serve hot or reheated. Makes 8 turnovers.

Sour Cream Pastry. Mix 2 cups unsifted all-purpose flour with ½ teaspoon salt, then finely cut in ½ cup (¼ lb.) butter or margarine. Beat 1 egg with ½ cup sour cream and stir into flour mixture until it holds together. Press dough into a ball.

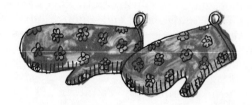

Ground Beef Spinach Crêpes

Wrap thin pancakes around a meat and spinach filling, then top each with tomato sauce and cheese before baking. You can fill them in advance and store, covered, in the refrigerator. Spoon over tomato sauce and cheese just before baking.

> 2 pounds lean ground beef
> 1 pound bulk pork sausage
> 2 medium-sized onions, finely chopped
> 3 cloves garlic, minced or mashed
> 4 packages (10 or 12 oz. each) frozen chopped
>   spinach, cooked and well drained
>   Salt to taste
> 6 eggs
> ¾ teaspoon salt
> 3 cups milk
> 2 cups regular all-purpose flour, unsifted
>   Butter or margarine
> 6 cans (8 oz. each) tomato sauce
> 2 cups shredded sharp Cheddar cheese

In a large frying pan over medium heat, sauté the beef and sausage with onion and garlic until meat is crumbly. Mix in spinach and salt to taste.

Beat eggs with the ¾ teaspoon salt and the milk. Stir flour into egg mixture; beat until well blended. Heat about ½ teaspoon butter in a 5 to 7-inch frying pan over medium-high heat; pour about 2 tablespoons batter into pan; tilt pan so batter covers bottom. When brown on bottom, turn and brown other side; lift out. Repeat this procedure until batter is used, buttering pan as needed.

Divide meat filling evenly between crêpes and roll each to enclose filling. Place seam side down in three 9 by 13-inch baking pans. (This much can be done ahead; cover and refrigerate.) Pour tomato sauce evenly over all the rolls; sprinkle evenly with cheese. Bake, uncovered, in a 350° oven for 30 minutes (40 to 45 minutes if refrigerated) or until cheese is bubbly and crêpes are heated through. Makes 18 to 27 servings of either 2 to 3 crêpes per serving.

Zucchini with Lamb Stuffing

Pick out zucchini 6 to 8 inches long for this main dish; plan on two halves for each serving.

> 4 zucchini (6 to 8 inches long)
>   Boiling salted water
> 1 pound lean ground lamb
> 2 tablespoons fine dry bread crumbs
> 1 tablespoon catsup
> ½ teaspoon meat seasoning sauce
>   or Worcestershire
> ¼ teaspoon garlic salt
> ⅛ teaspoon pepper
> ½ teaspoon salt
> 1 egg
> 3 tablespoons freshly grated Parmesan cheese

Cut off ends of zucchini and scrub well. Drop into the boiling water and cook until just slightly tender (about 5 minutes). Remove from heat and plunge zucchini into cold water; drain. When cool enough to handle, cut in half lengthwise and scoop out pulp with a spoon, leaving shell at least ¼ inch thick. Set shells aside. Mash or finely chop zucchini pulp and add lamb, crumbs, catsup, meat seasoning sauce, garlic salt, pepper, salt, and egg. Mix lightly; heap meat mixture into zucchini shells; arrange in a shallow baking dish. Sprinkle evenly with Parmesan cheese. Bake, uncovered, in a 350° oven for about 30 minutes or until well browned on top. Makes 4 servings.

Turkey Mushroom Turnovers

Frozen puff pastry is an easy step in making these tender turnovers.

> 2 tablespoons butter or margarine
> ½ pound thinly sliced mushrooms
> ½ cup sour cream
> 2 tablespoons all-purpose flour
> ½ teaspoon each salt and rubbed sage
> 1 pound ground turkey
> 1 package (10 oz.) frozen patty shells, thawed

In a large frying pan, melt the butter over medium-high heat; add mushrooms and sauté, stirring occasionally, until liquid has evaporated. In a small dish, stir together the sour cream, flour, salt, and sage; stir into mushrooms in pan and cook, stirring, until blended and bubbly. Turn mixture out into a bowl.

Rinse frying pan. Over high heat, cook turkey,

stirring to break up meat, until pinkness is gone (about 4 minutes). Stir meat and juices into mushroom mixture until blended. Set aside to cool to room temperature.

On a lightly floured board, roll each thawed patty shell into a circle about 7 inches in diameter. Divide turkey mixture into 6 equal portions. On half of each circle, place 1 portion turkey mixture. Moisten edges, fold rounds of dough in half, and seal edges together by pressing with tines of a fork. Place on ungreased, rimmed baking sheets. Bake in a 400° oven until pastry is well browned (about 35 minutes). Serve warm. Makes 6 turnovers.

Tourtière

From the French-speaking sections of Canada comes Tourtière, a savory pork pie with a flaky crust. The name is derived from the utensil used in making tourtes, **or large tarts.**

3 pounds lean ground pork, crumbled
1 small onion, finely chopped
1 cup finely chopped celery
1 clove garlic, minced or mashed
¼ cup each chopped parsley and celery leaves
1 bay leaf
1 teaspoon salt
¼ teaspoon each ground mace and
  marjoram leaves
⅛ teaspoon ground cloves
  Dash cayenne
  Tourtière Pastry (recipe follows)
2 slices French bread, crusts removed
2 tablespoons all-purpose flour
1 cup regular strength beef broth

In a large frying pan over medium heat, sauté pork with onion, celery, and garlic, stirring occasionally, until meat is browned and vegetables are soft. Blend in parsley, celery leaves, and seasonings. Simmer, uncovered, for about 30 minutes.

Meanwhile, line a 10-inch pie pan with half of the pastry. Whirl bread in blender to make fine crumbs; spread over bottom of pastry. Remove bay leaf and drain fat from pork mixture. Stir in flour; add broth, stirring until well blended. Cook until thickened and bubbly. Spread meat mixture in pastry-lined pan. Roll out remaining pastry for top crust; place over filling. Trim and flute edge of pastry; prick or slash top in several places. Bake in a 425° oven for 15 minutes, reduce heat to 350° and bake 25 to 30 minutes longer or until crust is well browned. Makes 8 servings.

Tourtière Pastry. Sift together 2 cups unsifted, regular all-purpose flour and ¾ teaspoon salt. Cut in ½ cup lard and 2 tablespoons butter. Stir in 1 egg beaten with 3 tablespoons cold water; shape dough into a ball. Chill at least 30 minutes; then roll out on a lightly floured board.

Beef and Spinach Casserole

You can assemble this casserole early in the day and hold in the refrigerator until ready to bake.

1 package (10 or 12 oz.) bow tie or butterfly-
    shaped noodles, cooked and warm
    Meat Sauce (recipe follows)
2 packages (10 or 12 oz. each) frozen chopped
    spinach, thawed and very well drained
2 cups (1 pt.) sour cream
1 cup grated or shredded Parmesan or
    Romano cheese

Combine noodles with Meat Sauce and let cool. Spread half the mixture over the bottom of a shallow 2½ to 3-quart casserole. Scatter half the spinach over noodles and dot evenly with half the sour cream, then spread gently to make an even layer. Sprinkle with half the cheese. Repeat layers of meat and noodles, spinach, and sour cream, and top evenly with remaining cheese. (Keep covered and cold until ready to bake.)

Bake, uncovered, in a 375° oven for 40 minutes or until heated through and top is lightly browned. Makes 6 to 8 servings.

Meat Sauce. Crumble ½ pound bulk pork sausage and 1 pound lean ground beef in a wide frying pan and cook over medium-high heat until meat loses pinkness. Add 1 large onion, chopped, and 1 clove garlic, minced. Cook, stirring occasionally, until vegetables are soft but not brown. Blend in 1 large can (15 oz.) tomato sauce, 1 can (6 oz.) tomato paste, 1½ cups water (or 1 cup dry red wine and ½ cup water), ¼ teaspoon *each* rosemary, basil, marjoram, oregano, and savory leaves, ¼ teaspoon black pepper, and about 1½ teaspoons salt (or to taste). Simmer slowly, uncovered, until reduced to about 6 cups (about 30 minutes).

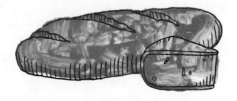

Stuffed Mushrooms

Stuff a savory sausage and beef mixture into large mushrooms (about 2½ inches in diameter) for this festive entrée.

¼ cup bulk pork sausage
1 medium-sized onion, finely chopped
1 clove garlic, minced or mashed
½ cup thinly sliced celery
¼ teaspoon each thyme leaves and rubbed sage
1 teaspoon oregano leaves, crushed
16 large mushrooms, about 2½ inches in diameter
1 pound lean ground beef
1 slice firm white bread
2 eggs
½ teaspoon salt
⅛ teaspoon pepper
¼ teaspoon Worcestershire
2 tablespoons butter or margarine
   Hot, cooked brown rice
   Chopped parsley for garnish (optional)

In a large frying pan, brown the sausage over medium-high heat. When sausage is brown and crumbly, add the onion, garlic, celery, thyme, sage, and oregano. Cook until onion is translucent (about 5 minutes).

Meanwhile, rinse mushrooms, remove and chop stems, set caps aside. Add stems and beef to the sausage and cook, stirring, until meat has lost all pinkness and most of the liquid is evaporated; cool slightly. Whirl bread in a blender to make ½ cup fine crumbs. Add to the meat, along with eggs, salt, pepper, and Worcestershire.

Place the butter in a 9 by 13-inch baking pan and set in the oven while it is preheating to 400°. Remove from oven as soon as the butter is melted. Turn the mushroom caps over in the butter until evenly coated. Mound about ¼ cup of the meat mixture in each mushroom and arrange the filled mushrooms in the baking pan. Bake, uncovered, in a 400° oven for 15 to 20 minutes or until browned.

To serve, pile the cooked rice in the center of a serving plate and arrange the mushrooms around it. Garnish with chopped parsley, if desired. Makes 8 servings of 2 mushrooms each.

Potato Topped Beef Loaf

Pat this seasoned meat loaf into a round casserole and top with frozen potato puffs. You can shape it now and bake later.

2 tablespoons butter or margarine
1 package (1 lb.) frozen diced onions, thawed
   (or 1½ cups chopped onions)
½ cup milk
1 egg
1½ slices firm white bread, broken in pieces
1 teaspoon each salt and Worcestershire
¼ teaspoon thyme leaves
2 cloves garlic, minced
1½ pounds lean ground beef
1 can (10½ oz.) condensed cream of mushroom soup, undiluted
1 package (1 lb.) frozen potato puffs

Melt butter in a large frying pan over medium heat; add onions, and sauté until golden brown, stirring; set aside. Combine in a blender the milk, egg, bread, salt, Worcestershire, thyme, and garlic; whirl until smooth. Place the meat in a large bowl, pour in the milk mixture, and mix lightly. Pat into a greased 2-quart casserole (9 or 10 inches in diameter). Spoon over the onions and mushroom soup, making an even layer. (Refrigerate at this point, if made ahead.)

Arrange frozen potato puffs on top. Bake, uncovered, in a 400° oven for 40 minutes (about 65 minutes if refrigerated) or until potatoes are well browned and meat is cooked through to your liking when slashed. Cut in wedges. Makes 6 servings.

Quick Baked Chile

On a winter evening offer steaming bowls of this well seasoned chile with a crisp green salad and crusty bread.

1 tablespoon salad oil
1 pound lean ground beef
½ cup chopped celery
1 medium-sized onion, chopped
1 can (10¾ oz.) condensed tomato soup
1 can (15 oz.) kidney beans
¾ cup water
1 tablespoon paprika
2 teaspoons chile powder
⅛ teaspoon each garlic powder and ground allspice
½ cup shredded sharp Cheddar cheese

In a medium-sized frying pan, heat the oil over medium-high heat and crumble in the ground beef. Brown meat well. Add the celery and onion; sauté until onion is soft. Blend in the tomato soup, kidney beans and their liquid, water, paprika, chile powder, garlic powder, and allspice. Pour into an ungreased 1½-quart casserole. Cover and bake in a 350° oven for 30 to 45 minutes until chile is hot and bubbly.

Uncover, skim off any fat, sprinkle cheese over top, and return to oven until cheese melts (5 to 10 minutes). Makes 4 servings.

Chile Beef and Cornbread Casserole

On a summer evening you might serve this with a mixed green salad, a pitcher of iced tea or sangria, and slices of melon for dessert.

    1 green pepper
    3 pounds lean ground beef
    1 tablespoon salad oil
    2 large onions, finely chopped
    2 cloves garlic, minced or mashed
    1 tablespoon chile powder
    ½ teaspoon each celery salt, pepper, and ground
        cumin seed
    2 teaspoons salt
    1 can (12 oz.) whole kernel corn with sweet
        peppers, drained
    1 can (10 oz.) red chile sauce
    1 large can (15 oz.) tomato sauce
    1 package (about 15 oz.) cornbread mix

Remove both ends from green pepper and discard seeds. Cut 3 thin rings, each about ¼ inch thick, and set aside for garnish; finely chop the remaining pepper.

Cook the lean ground beef in the oil in a large frying pan or Dutch oven over medium-high heat until brown and crumbly. Add the chopped green pepper, onions, and garlic. Cook until onion is limp (about 3 minutes). Stir in chile powder, celery salt, pepper, cumin, salt, corn, chile sauce, and tomato sauce. Let meat sauce simmer, uncovered, for 15 minutes. (Cool, cover, and chill if made ahead.)

Skim or lift off fat from meat sauce and discard. (If meat sauce was chilled, reheat to simmering.) Pour into a greased 9 by 13-inch baking pan.

Prepare the cornbread mix as directed on the package. Spread cornbread batter over hot meat sauce. Bake, uncovered, in a 400° oven until bread is lightly browned (about 25 minutes). Garnish top with green pepper rings. Cut in squares and lift pieces out with a spatula; spoon any remaining sauce over bread. Makes 8 to 10 servings.

Corn Chip Chile

You can assemble this chile ahead, ready to heat in the oven just before serving.

    3 cans (15 oz. each) red kidney beans, drained
    2 cans (about 10 oz. each) enchilada sauce
    2 cups shredded Cheddar cheese
    1½ tablespoons chile powder
    1 package (5 oz.) corn chips
    1½ pounds lean ground beef
    1½ cups chopped onions
    1 clove garlic, minced
    2 tablespoons salad oil or olive oil
        Sour cream

Combine the kidney beans, enchilada sauce, Cheddar cheese, chile powder, and corn chips. In a frying pan over medium-high heat, sauté ground beef, onions, and garlic in oil until meat is brown and onions are tender. Discard any fat. Stir together meat and bean mixture; pour into a 3-quart baking dish, and bake, uncovered, in a 350° oven for about 30 minutes until hot and bubbly. Remove from oven, top with dollops of sour cream. Return to oven and heat for 5 minutes longer. Makes 8 to 10 servings.

Syrian-Style Stuffed Whole Cabbage

Choose a fairly large, loose-leafed head of fresh new spring cabbage or use curly-leaf, dark green Savoy cabbage. Select a head that's about 2¼ to 2½ pounds. Avoid small heavy heads with tight compact leaves.

1 *loose-leafed head (about 2¼ to 2½ lbs.)*
   new green or Savoy cabbage
   Boiling water
1 *tablespoon butter or margarine*
½ *cup pine nuts*
¼ *pound mushrooms, chopped*
1 *medium-sized onion, chopped*
2 *cloves garlic, minced or mashed*
1½ *pounds lean ground lamb*
3 *tablespoons soy sauce*
1 *teaspoon dry mustard*
1 *teaspoon each rubbed sage and*
   thyme leaves
¼ *cup catsup*
⅓ *cup fine dry bread crumbs*
1 *egg*
   About 4 to 5 cups hot cooked rice
   Chopped parsley for garnish
   About 1½ cups unflavored yogurt

To prepare cabbage, trim off core if it extends beyond head; then carefully hollow out just the center of the core about 1 inch deep. Remove and discard torn outer leaves. Place cabbage, core end down, in the middle of several layers of cheesecloth (each 25 to 30 inches long). Pull up the four corners of cloth and tie close to the top of the head with string. In a large kettle (about 10 to 12-qt. size), bring to boiling enough water to cover cabbage.

Immerse head and simmer until a thin skewer inserted through the top of the cabbage comes out easily; it takes about 12 minutes for new green cabbage or 7 minutes for Savoy. With a spoon, turn head over frequently while cooking. With tongs, lift cabbage from water and let drain in a colander. When cool enough to handle, place cabbage on a board; untie and fold back cheesecloth but leave it in place. Begin folding back the leaves one by one until cabbage resembles a large rose.

For the filling, melt butter in a small frying pan over low heat. Add pine nuts and cook, stirring, until golden; set aside. In a large frying pan, over medium-high heat, cook mushrooms, onions, and garlic until onion is limp. Remove from heat; cool slightly, then combine in a bowl with the lamb, soy, mustard, sage, thyme, catsup, crumbs, egg, and pine nuts (reserve 1 tablespoon for garnish). Mix well.

To stuff cabbage, start with about 1 tablespoon filling, pat into a ball, and tuck it into the very center of the head. Press a layer of the surrounding leaves firmly around the meat. Then start putting the leaves back in place with a layer of filling between each layer of leaves. The easiest way is to pick up 1 or 2 tablespoons of filling at a time, poke some down by the base of the leaf, then pat a fairly even layer of it over the back of one leaf before covering it with the next leaf.

Gradually increase the amount of filling as you fill the larger leaves. Try to use up the filling when all but the last 2 or 3 layers of leaves have been filled. Bring these final layers, without filling, upward and press them around the head. Then bring up the corners of cheesecloth and tie again close to the head. You could do this much ahead and refrigerate.

To steam the cabbage, you'll need to put some kind of rack in the bottom of the kettle to support the head over about 1½ inches of boiling water (you might rest a small cooling rack on something like a tuna can with both ends removed). Place cabbage in steamer above (but not touching) rapidly boiling water, cover kettle tightly, and steam for 50 minutes (or 1 hour if refrigerated), replacing boiling water as needed. Lift cabbage from steamer with heavy tongs and cool on a plate for about 10 minutes.

Meanwhile, arrange hot rice in a rimmed serving dish. Untie cheesecloth and, using a wide spatula, carefully lift cabbage and place it on the rice. Pour any juices that accumulated on the plate over the cabbage.

To serve, garnish cabbage top with reserved pine nuts and parsley. Cut cabbage into thick wedges and lift wedges onto plates with a pie server or narrow spatula. Pass a bowl of yogurt at the table to spoon over each serving. Makes 4 to 6 servings.

Garbanzo Bean Casserole

Canned garbanzos and sliced water chestnuts spark this unusual casserole. A sprinkling of Cheddar cheese is added just before it goes into the oven.

  1 tablespoon salad oil
1½ pounds lean ground beef
  ½ teaspoon each salt, pepper, and garlic salt
  2 large onions, chopped
  1 can (about 1 lb. 12 oz.) tomatoes
  2 cans (about 1 lb. each) garbanzo beans, drained
  1 can (about 5 oz.) water chestnuts, drained
     and sliced
  ½ cup shredded sharp Cheddar cheese

Heat the oil in a large frying pan (one with a cover) over medium heat; add the ground beef and cook until brown and crumbly. Add the salt, pepper, garlic salt, and onions and sauté until onion is limp. Stir in tomatoes (break up with a fork) and their liquid, cover, and simmer for 30 minutes. Add beans and water chestnuts to meat mixture and stir until well blended. Pour into a 2½-quart casserole. Sprinkle the cheese on top and bake, uncovered, in a 350° oven for about 30 minutes or until lightly browned. Makes 6 to 8 servings.

Western Meal-in-One

Assemble this in the morning and refrigerate; then allow 1½ hours for baking.

  1 pound lean ground beef
  1 tablespoon salad oil
  1 clove garlic, minced or mashed
  1 teaspoon salt
  1 large onion, finely chopped
  1 green pepper, seeded and chopped
  1 teaspoon chile powder
  1 can (1 lb.) tomatoes
  1 can (1 lb.) kidney beans
  ¾ cup uncooked rice
  ¼ cup chopped ripe olives
  ¾ cup shredded Cheddar cheese

In a frying pan over medium heat, brown ground beef in oil until crumbly. Add garlic, salt, onion, and green pepper; sauté 5 minutes or until vegetables are limp. Mix in chile powder, tomatoes (break up with a spoon) and their liquid, kidney beans and their liquid, and rice and turn into a greased 2-quart casserole. (This

much can be done ahead; cover and refrigerate.) Bake, uncovered, in a 350° oven for 45 minutes. Sprinkle with olives and cheese and continue baking for 15 minutes longer or until cheese is melted. (If refrigerated, allow 1½ hours total.) Makes 8 servings.

Miniature Beef Turnovers

Making these small turnovers takes some time, but you can do it ahead, freeze the baked pastries, and reheat them just before serving.

  ½ teaspoon salt
  ½ pound lean ground beef
  ⅓ cup chopped onion
  ¼ cup finely chopped mushrooms
  ¼ teaspoon dill weed
  ⅛ teaspoon pepper
  3 tablespoons sour cream
  1 cup (½ lb.) soft butter
  1 cup small curd cottage cheese
  2 cups regular all-purpose flour, unsifted

Heat the salt in a frying pan over medium heat; add the ground beef and chopped onion, and cook until beef is brown and crumbly (about 7 minutes). Stir in the mushrooms, dill weed, pepper, and sour cream. Blend well; set aside.

In an electric mixer bowl, beat together the butter and cottage cheese until smooth and creamy. Add the flour and beat until thoroughly combined.

Roll out half the dough at a time on a floured pastry cloth or board into a rectangle that is 10 by 16 inches (about ⅛ inch thick). Cut dough into 2-inch squares. Spoon about ¼ teaspoon of

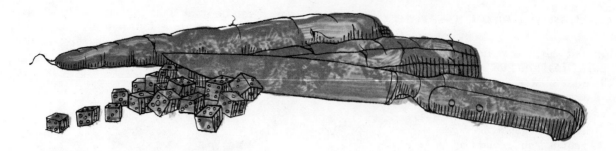

the filling on one corner of each square; bring the opposite corner over top to enclose the filling. With a fork, press the open edges together to seal. Arrange turnovers about 1 inch apart on ungreased baking sheets. Bake in a 350° oven for 15 to 18 minutes or until pastry is lightly browned. Serve hot or store turnovers by cooling, wrapping airtight, and freezing. (If baked ahead and frozen, reheat, uncovered, in a 350° oven about 10 minutes.) Makes 80 appetizers.

Layered Vegetable Beef Casserole

A can of soup provides the shortcut sauce for this herb seasoned casserole.

2 pounds lean ground beef
2 medium-sized onions, chopped
1 teaspoon fines herbes (or ¼ teaspoon each oregano, thyme, rosemary, and basil leaves)
½ teaspoon seasoned salt
¼ teaspoon each seasoned pepper and ground nutmeg
⅛ teaspoon garlic powder
1½ pounds zucchini
4 medium-sized carrots
About 1 cup boiling salted water
1 can (10½ oz.) condensed cream of mushroom soup
12 square slices (12 oz.) process American cheese

Sauté the meat, onion, fines herbes, salt, pepper, nutmeg, and garlic powder in a frying pan over medium heat, stirring, until meat loses its pinkness. Cut zucchini and carrots in ¼-inch slices. Cook zucchini in salted water until just tender (about 4 minutes). With a slotted spoon, place in a bowl. Return water to boiling and cook carrots until just tender (about 6 minutes); drain. Mix zucchini with the mushroom soup and put half of the mixture in a greased 3-quart baking dish. Top with half the carrots, half the meat mixture, and 6 slices of cheese. Repeat layers. Bake, uncovered, in a 350° oven for about 30

minutes or until heated through. Makes 6 to 8 servings.

Macaroni, Sicilian-Style

A variety of garden vegetables combine in this hearty well seasoned casserole making it a good choice for a one dish meal to feed a hungry group.

1½ pounds lean ground beef
2 tablespoons salad oil
4 medium-sized carrots, diced
1 large onion, chopped
¼ pound mushrooms, sliced
2 cans (6 oz. each) tomato paste
1 can (1 lb.) tomatoes
⅔ cup dry Sherry or water
1½ teaspoons each salt, sugar, basil leaves, and oregano leaves
½ teaspoon each pepper and garlic powder
1 package (10 or 12 oz.) frozen chopped spinach
6 ounces small elbow macaroni
1½ cups shredded Cheddar cheese

In a large frying pan over medium heat, cook ground beef in oil until crumbly. Add carrots, onion, and mushrooms; sauté, stirring often, for about 5 minutes. Add tomato paste, tomatoes (breaking them up with a spoon) and their liquid, Sherry, and seasonings. Cook slowly, uncovered, for 30 minutes, stirring often. Meanwhile, thaw spinach and cook macaroni according to package directions. Drain macaroni and spinach well; mix together.

Put half the macaroni mixture in a greased 9 by 13-inch baking pan; top with half the meat sauce and ½ cup of the cheese.

Repeat layers of macaroni and meat sauce, then sprinkle remaining 1 cup cheese on top. (This much can be done ahead; cover and chill.) Bake, uncovered, in a 375° oven for about 30 minutes or until heated through (45 to 50 minutes if refrigerated). Makes 8 to 10 servings.

Ground Beef and Corn Pie

Line a pie dish with the seasoned ground beef, then fill it with a spicy corn mixture.

1 *pound lean ground beef*
¼ *cup each fine dry bread crumbs and catsup*
2 *tablespoons finely chopped onion*
1 *small clove garlic, minced or mashed*
½ *teaspoon salt*
2 *teaspoons chile powder*
⅛ *teaspoon pepper*
2 *eggs*
¼ *cup milk*
   Dash liquid hot pepper seasoning
1 *can (about 8 oz.) cream-style corn*
¼ *cup seeded and chopped green pepper*
½ *cup each shredded Cheddar cheese and grated*
   Parmesan cheese
   Pitted ripe olives (optional)

Combine the meat with crumbs, catsup, onion, garlic, salt, chile powder, and pepper; mix with your hands until well blended. Pat the meat mixture lightly and evenly over the bottom and sides of a 9-inch pie pan (at least 1½ inches deep). Beat the eggs slightly with the milk and hot pepper seasoning. Stir in the corn and green pepper. Pour into center of pie. Bake, uncovered, in a 375° oven for about 35 minutes or until corn mixture is set. Combine the Cheddar and Parmesan cheese and sprinkle over pie. Return to oven for about 5 minutes until cheese melts. Garnish the top with pitted ripe olives before serving, if you wish. Makes 4 servings.

Khorake Bademjan

This Persian combination of layered eggplant and ground beef resembles moussaka.

2 *medium-sized eggplants*
   Salt
   About ¾ cup butter or margarine
2 *large onions, thinly sliced*
1½ *pounds lean ground beef*
2 *small cloves garlic, minced*
½ *teaspoon each ground nutmeg and cinnamon*
   Salt and pepper
3 *medium-sized tomatoes, peeled and sliced*
   Paprika
   Yogurt or sour cream

Cut each eggplant in half lengthwise, then cut each section across in ½-inch-thick slices. Generously sprinkle eggplant with salt and let stand for at least 30 minutes; rinse slices in clear water and dry thoroughly.

Melt enough butter in a wide frying pan to coat bottom. Cook eggplant slices, without crowding, over medium heat until lightly browned; add more butter to pan as needed. Drain the cooked slices.

In the same pan melt the balance of the butter (or at least 2 tablespoons) and cook the onions, stirring, until soft.

Set onions aside and put in the pan the meat, garlic, nutmeg, and cinnamon. Crumble meat and cook over high heat, stirring constantly until it loses pinkness and all the juices are evaporated. Add salt and pepper to taste.

Arrange half the cooked eggplant slices over the bottom of a large, ungreased casserole (about 3-quart size). Spoon the seasoned meat over the eggplant, then cover with sliced tomatoes. Top with the remaining cooked eggplant and spread onions over all. Dust top liberally with paprika. Bake immediately or refrigerate, covered, until ready to heat.

Cover casserole and bake in a 375° oven for 20 minutes (30 to 40 minutes if refrigerated) or until heated through. Top individual servings with a dollop of yogurt or sour cream. Makes about 6 servings.

Beef and Eggplant Casserole

If you're ready for a bit of instant Middle East, try this simplified version of moussaka that can be prepared ahead. Serve with crusty rolls or French bread.

1 *medium eggplant (about 1½ lbs.)*
2 *tablespoons salad oil*
   Water
1½ *pounds lean ground beef*
1 *large onion, chopped*
1 *can (8 oz.) tomato sauce*
1½ *teaspoons seasoned salt*
½ *teaspoon seasoned pepper*
1 *tablespoon Worcestershire*
2 *cups thinly shredded cabbage*
8 *ounces Longhorn Cheddar cheese, shredded*

Wash and dice eggplant. Using a large frying pan that can be covered, heat oil over medium-high heat. Put in eggplant and cook, stirring, about 15 minutes. Add 2 tablespoons water, cover, and cook; every few minutes uncover pan, stir, and add water a tablespoon at a time as needed until eggplant is tender. Turn into a greased 2-quart casserole. Brown the meat in the frying pan until crumbly; add onion and cook until limp. Stir in tomato sauce, 2 tablespoons water, salt, pepper, Worcestershire, and cabbage. Cover and simmer 10 minutes.

Mix meat mixture and 1½ cups of the cheese into casserole. Sprinkle with remaining cheese. (This much can be done ahead;cover and chill.)

Bake, uncovered, in a 350° oven for 30 minutes (about 1 hour if refrigerated) or until heated through. Makes about 6 servings.

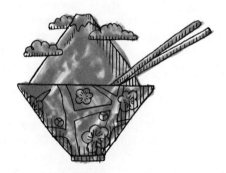

Oriental Beef Casserole

The separate layers of this dish retain their identity and remain crisp and colorful.

  1 *package (7 oz.) frozen edible-pod peas*
  1 *pound lean ground beef*
  1 *medium-sized onion, chopped*
    Butter or margarine
  1 *can (10½ oz.) condensed cream of*
     mushroom soup
  3 *tablespoons milk*
  1 *tablespoon soy sauce*
 ⅛ *teaspoon pepper*
  1 *can (3 oz.) chow mein noodles*

Allow the pod peas to thaw at room temperature about an hour. In a frying pan over medium-high heat, sauté the ground beef and chopped onion, adding butter if needed; cook until brown and crumbly. Spoon meat into a greased shallow 1½-quart casserole. Arrange the thawed peas over the browned meat. Combine the mushroom soup with the milk, soy sauce, and pepper; pour over the peas and meat. Sprinkle top with the crisp noodles. Bake, uncovered, in a 375° oven for 25 to 30 minutes or until heated through. Makes 4 to 6 servings.

Ground Beef and Olive Casserole

As this casserole bakes, the pitted olives become stuffed with the meaty sauce. You can assemble it ahead; bake just before serving.

  2 *pounds lean ground beef*
  1 *large onion, chopped*
  2 *cloves garlic, minced or mashed*
 1½ *teaspoons salt*
 ¼ *teaspoon pepper*
  1 *tablespoon chile powder*
  1 *can (6 or 8 oz.) sliced mushrooms*
  2 *cans (8 oz. each) tomato sauce*
  1 *large can (7½ oz.) pitted ripe olives, drained*
  2 *cups shredded sharp Cheddar cheese*
  6 *ounces wide egg noodles*
    Boiling salted water

In a large frying pan over medium heat, cook the ground beef and onions together, stirring, until the meat has lost its pinkness; add the garlic, salt, pepper, and chile powder as the meat cooks. Add mushrooms (including their liquid), tomato sauce, and olives; cover and simmer 20 minutes. Remove from heat, then add 1½ cups of the cheese and stir until melted.

Meanwhile, cook the noodles in boiling water as directed on the package; drain. Arrange half the cooked noodles in a 9 by 13-inch baking pan and cover with half the meat sauce. Repeat layers with remaining noodles and sauce. Sprinkle remaining cheese on top. (This much can be done ahead; cover and chill.) Bake, uncovered, in a 350° oven for 20 minutes or until heated through. (If refrigerated, bake, covered, for 45 minutes; remove cover and bake 15 minutes more.) Makes 8 servings.

Baked Beans with Beef

If you have a meaty ham bone, use it instead of the ham hock in this recipe.

 ½ *pound large white (Great Northern) dried beans*
    About 3 cups water
  1 *ham hock (about 1 lb.)*
  1 *tablespoon butter or salad oil*
  2 *medium-sized onions, sliced*
  1 *pound lean ground beef*
  1 *large can (1 lb. 12 oz.) pear-shaped tomatoes*
  2 *tablespoons firmly packed brown sugar*
  1 *tablespoon each dry mustard, mustard seed,*
     and chile powder.
  1 *teaspoon Worcestershire*
    Salt and pepper to taste

Wash beans and put into a heavy pan with 3 cups water. Bring to boiling and boil 2 minutes; then cover, remove from heat, and soak beans for 1 hour.

Without draining beans, add ham hock to pan; cover and simmer until beans are tender (about 1 hour), adding more water if needed. Remove ham bone, pick off any meat and add to beans; discard bone and fat. Meanwhile, heat butter in a frying pan over medium heat and sauté onions; remove from pan. In the same pan, cook beef, stirring until crumbly. Add tomatoes (break up with a spoon) and their liquid, sugar, mustard, mustard seed, chile powder, and Worcestershire; simmer, uncovered, for 10 minutes; combine with beans in a 2½-quart casserole. Add salt and pepper to taste; stir in onions. Bake, uncovered, in a 400° oven for about 30 minutes or until heated through. Makes 6 servings.

Zucchini-Ground Beef Casserole

If you like a casserole with a crusty, cheese-flavored topping, this is it. You can prepare it a day ahead and then bake it just before serving.

    1 pound lean ground beef
    1 medium-sized onion, chopped
    1 tablespoon salad oil
    1 can (1 lb. 12 oz.) tomatoes
    1 can (8 oz.) tomato sauce
    1 can (6 oz.) tomato paste
    1 small green pepper, seeded and chopped
    ¼ pound (1 cup) shredded sharp Cheddar cheese
    6 medium-sized zucchini, sliced ½ inch thick
    ½ cup pitted ripe olives
    ½ teaspoon salt
      Freshly ground pepper to taste
    ¼ teaspoon garlic salt
    ⅛ teaspoon oregano leaves
    ½ to ¾ cup grated Parmesan cheese

Sauté meat and onion together in salad oil in a large frying pan over medium heat until meat is browned and crumbly. Add tomatoes (break up with a spoon) and their liquid, tomato sauce, tomato paste, green pepper, Cheddar cheese, zucchini, and olives. Season with salt, pepper, garlic salt, and oregano. Simmer, uncovered, for 10 minutes. Turn into an 8 by 12-inch baking pan and sprinkle generously with the Parmesan cheese. (This much can be done ahead; cover and refrigerate as long as overnight.) Bake, uncovered, in a 350° oven for 1 hour (1½ hours if refrigerated) until the sauce is bubbly and the top is nicely browned and slightly crusty. Makes 8 servings.

Spicy Lamb Balls with Rice

Seasoned with gingersnaps, these meatballs bake on top of a flavorful rice mixture.

    1 can (10½ oz.) condensed beef consommé
    1 cup water
    1 cup long grain rice (uncooked)
    1½ pounds lean ground lamb
    1 teaspoon garlic powder
    ¼ teaspoon salt
    ⅛ teaspoon pepper
    ⅓ cup finely crushed gingersnaps
    2 tablespoons soy sauce
    1 egg
    2 tablespoons chopped chives or green onions
    1 can (8 oz.) stewed tomatoes

In a saucepan, combine consommé and water; bring to boiling, add rice, cover, and simmer for 20 minutes or until liquid is absorbed. Turn into a shallow, 2½-quart casserole. Meanwhile, in a bowl combine the lamb, garlic powder, salt, pepper, gingersnap crumbs, soy sauce, and egg. Mix lightly to blend. Shape the meat into balls about the size of golf balls. Arrange on a shallow baking pan and bake, uncovered, in a 500° oven for 7 to 9 minutes or until no longer pink inside when slashed. Spoon meatballs on top of rice; sprinkle with chives. Break up tomatoes with a fork; pour over meat. (This much can be done ahead; cover and refrigerate.)

Bake, covered, in a 350° oven for 20 minutes (about 40 minutes if refrigerated) or until bubbly. Makes 4 to 6 servings.

Full Meal Soups: Hearty and Robust

Beef and Carrot Soup

While the beef and vegetables simmer, prepare the cream sauce. Then combine the two mixtures just before serving.

> 1 pound lean ground beef
> 1½ cups coarsely chopped onion (about 3 medium-sized onions)
> 6 cups water
> 1½ cups coarsely grated carrot (about 4 medium-sized carrots)
>   About 1½ teaspoons salt
>   About ½ teaspoon pepper
> 4 tablespoons (⅛ lb.) butter or margarine
> ⅓ cup all-purpose flour
> 1½ cups milk
>   Grated Parmesan cheese

In a large frying pan over medium-high heat, sauté beef and onion together for 5 minutes, stirring with a fork to crumble meat. While meat is browning, heat water to boiling in a 5-quart kettle, then add meat, onion, pan drippings, carrot, 1½ teaspoons salt, and ½ teaspoon pepper. Cover and simmer for 1 hour. Melt butter in a saucepan;

blend in flour until smooth; add milk and cook, stirring constantly, until smooth and thick. Just before serving, stir the cream sauce into the ground beef mixture and heat. Taste, and add salt and pepper if needed. Sprinkle 1 tablespoon grated cheese over each serving. Serves 6 to 8.

Armenian Soup

Quick-cooking cracked wheat gives an interesting texture to the miniature meatballs. Offer small bowls of the egg-enriched broth and meatballs as a first course or with a sandwich for lunch.

> ½ pound lean ground beef
> ½ cup quick-cooking cracked wheat
> ¼ cup each finely chopped onion and parsley
> 5 cans (14 oz. each) regular strength chicken broth or 1½ large cans (46 oz. size)
> ⅓ cup lemon juice
> 3 eggs
>   Salt and pepper to taste

Combine ground beef with cracked wheat, onion, and parsley; form into tiny balls about the size of filbert nuts. In a 5-quart kettle, heat the chicken broth to boiling and drop in meatballs; simmer, covered, for about ½ hour. Just before you are ready to serve, combine lemon juice with eggs in a large heat-proof bowl; beat until thoroughly blended. Using a slotted spoon, remove meatballs from broth and distribute among individual soup bowls. Slowly pour hot broth into egg mixture, beating constantly. Taste, adding salt and pepper if needed. Ladle into bowls and serve immediately. Makes 10 to 12 servings.

Meatball Soup with Swiss Chard and Red Peppers

Moist, tender meatballs poach in the liquid of this quickly assembled soup. Sweetly flavored red peppers and fresh Swiss chard are the preferred vegetables to use in it, but if they're hard to find, use instead green peppers and frozen Swiss chard.

    2 *large onions, chopped*
    2 *large red bell (or green) peppers, seeded*
       and chopped
    1 *cup chopped parsley*
    3 *tablespoons olive oil or salad oil*
    ¼ *cup uncooked rice*
    4 *cups regular strength chicken or beef broth*
    4 *cups water*
    1 *pound Swiss chard or 2 packages (12 oz. each)*
       frozen Swiss chard, thawed
 1½ *pounds lean ground beef*
    1 *egg*
    ¼ *cup all-purpose flour*
    ½ *cup milk*
    1 *teaspoon salt*
       Sour cream

In a 5 or 6-quart kettle, combine the onions, peppers, parsley, and oil. Cook over medium-high heat, stirring, until vegetables are soft but not browned. Add the rice, broth, and water (or use all broth in place of water).

Cut white stems from Swiss chard and chop; add to soup. Chop chard leaves and set aside. (If frozen Swiss chard is used, stir into soup after it has cooked 10 minutes).

Thoroughly mix together the ground beef, egg, flour, milk, and salt. Shape meat with hands into balls about 1 inch in diameter, dropping as formed into soup. Bring soup to a boil, cover, and simmer gently 10 minutes.

Remove lid and stir in Swiss chard leaves, cover and simmer 10 minutes more. Serve hot or chill and reheat to serve. Pass sour cream to add, if desired, to individual portions. Makes about 4½ quarts or 9 main dish servings of 2-cup size.

Cabbage Patch Soup

A topping of mashed potatoes perches on each serving of this hearty supper soup.

    1 *pound lean ground beef*
    2 *tablespoons butter or margarine*
    1 *medium-sized onion, thinly sliced*
    ½ *cup thinly sliced celery*
    1 *can (1 lb.) tomatoes*
    2 *cups water*
    1 *can (1 lb.) red kidney beans*
    1 *teaspoon each salt and chile powder*
    ⅛ *teaspoon pepper*
    2 *cups thinly shredded cabbage*
       Mashed Potato Topping (recipe follows)

In a large frying pan or Dutch oven over medium-high heat, cook the beef in butter, stirring until browned and crumbly. Add onion and celery and sauté about 5 minutes. Discard any fat. Stir in tomatoes and their liquid (break up tomatoes with a fork), water, beans and their liquid, salt, chile powder, and pepper. Bring to boiling, add cabbage, cover, and cook until cabbage is tender (about 3 minutes). Serve in soup plates or large bowls with a mound of the Mashed Potato Topping. Makes 4 to 6 servings.

Mashed Potato Topping. Prepare enough instant mashed potatoes for 4 servings following directions for stiff potatoes; beat in about 1 tablespoon instant toasted minced onion.

Sausage Bean Soup

Fresh mushrooms and tomatoes enhance this main dish soup.

    1 *pound dried small white beans*
    2 *quarts cold water*
 1½ *pounds bulk pork sausage*
    1 *large onion, chopped*
    1 *cup sliced mushrooms*
    3 *medium-sized fresh tomatoes, peeled*
       and chopped
    1 *teaspoon salt*
    ¼ *teaspoon pepper*
       Sour cream (optional)

(Continued on next page)

Wash and pick over beans and put into a Dutch oven or other large pan. Pour over the water. Cover and bring to boiling; boil for 2 minutes, remove from heat, and allow to soak for 1 hour or longer. Without draining beans, return to boiling; reduce heat and simmer, covered, for 1½ hours.

Meanwhile, crumble the sausage into a frying pan over medium heat; sauté, stirring, until browned; remove with a slotted spoon and add to beans. Discard all except about 2 tablespoons of the sausage drippings in frying pan. Add onion and mushrooms and sauté over medium heat until lightly browned. After the beans have cooked 1½ hours, add the sautéed vegetables, tomatoes, salt, and pepper. Cover and cook about 30 minutes longer or until beans are tender. Top each serving with sour cream, if you wish. Makes about 6 servings.

Greek Meatball Soup

Tiny meatballs simmer in and enrich the stock of this hearty cheese-flavored soup.

  2 tablespoons butter or margarine
  ¾ cup finely chopped onion
  6 cups water
  ¼ cup beef stock base (or 12 beef bouillon cubes)
  1 pound lean ground beef
  2 tablespoons uncooked rice
  1 clove garlic, minced
  ½ teaspoon salt
  ⅛ teaspoon oregano leaves, crumbled
  ½ cup finely chopped parsley
  2 tablespoons cornstarch blended with
    2 tablespoons cold water
  ½ cup whipping cream
  ½ cup shredded Parmesan cheese
  1 bunch green onions, finely chopped
    Shredded Parmesan cheese

Melt butter in a large sauce pan (about 3-quart size) over medium heat; add onions and cook, stirring until golden brown. Remove a third of the onions from the pan and set aside. Pour in water and stock base, cover, and simmer while shaping meatballs.

Mix together the ground beef, reserved sautéed onions, rice, garlic, salt, and oregano and shape into marble-sized balls. Roll in parsley and drop into the bubbling stock. Cover and simmer 25 minutes. Stir cornstarch mixture into simmering soup. Mix together cream and the ½ cup shredded cheese; ladle about 1 cup hot stock into the cheese mixture; then return all to pan. Cook, stirring,

until heated through. Serve with bowls of green onions and shredded cheese to spoon over. Makes 4 to 6 servings.

Meatball Vegetable Soup

Conveniently, this richly flavored soup is very good reheated. You can prepare the full recipe and then freeze any extra soup for a future meal.

  1 large beef knucklebone
  2 or 3 marrow bones
  ½ cup pearl barley
    About 2 quarts water
  1 can (1 lb. 12 oz.) tomatoes, cut in pieces
  1 pound lean ground beef
  ½ cup cracker meal
  1 egg
  2 teaspoons salt
  ½ teaspoon pepper
  4 medium-sized carrots, sliced
  3 stalks celery with tops, sliced
  1 medium-sized onion, chopped
  2 cloves garlic, minced or mashed
  2 small zucchini, thinly sliced
  ½ cup fresh or frozen peas

Place the knucklebone, marrow bones, pearl barley, and 2 quarts water in a large kettle; cover and simmer for 3 hours. Discard bones and skim fat from broth. Add enough water to make 2 quarts total liquid. Add tomatoes and their liquid, cover, and simmer slowly while you prepare meatballs. Mix together the beef, cracker meal, egg, 1 teaspoon of the salt, and ¼ teaspoon of the pepper. Shape into tiny meatballs about 1 inch in diameter and drop into simmering broth. Add carrots, celery, onion, garlic, and remaining 1 teaspoon salt and ¼ teaspoon pepper. Cover and cook slowly for 45 minutes. Add sliced zucchini and peas and continue cooking for 15 minutes more. Makes 8 to 10 servings.

Hamburger Soup

Serve this main dish soup with hot, crusty bread for a family lunch or supper.

2 pounds lean ground beef
2 tablespoons olive oil or salad oil
⅓ cup dried split peas
½ teaspoon salt
¼ teaspoon each pepper, oregano leaves, and
    basil leaves
⅛ teaspoon seasoned salt
1 package onion soup mix (enough for
    4 servings)
6 cups boiling water
1 can (8 oz.) tomato sauce
1 tablespoon soy sauce
1 cup thinly sliced celery
¼ cup celery leaves, torn in large pieces
1 cup thinly sliced carrots
1 cup elbow macaroni
    Freshly grated Parmesan cheese

In a large saucepan or kettle with a tight fitting lid, brown meat in oil over medium-high heat. Discard any fat. Add split peas, salt, pepper, oregano, basil, seasoned salt, and onion soup mix. Stir in boiling water, tomato sauce, and soy sauce. Cover and simmer for about 25 minutes. Meanwhile, prepare celery, celery leaves, and carrots; then add to simmering mixture and continue to cook, covered, for 15 minutes longer. Add macaroni, cover and cook 12 to 15 minutes or until macaroni is tender. Pass grated Parmesan cheese to be sprinkled over individual servings. Makes 6 to 8 servings.

Eggplant Supper Soup

Ground beef, macaroni, and vegetables all are combined here to make a hearty soup reminiscent of Italian minestrone.

2 tablespoons each salad oil and butter
    or margarine
1 medium-sized onion, chopped
1 pound lean ground beef
1 medium-sized eggplant, diced
1 clove garlic, minced or mashed
½ cup each chopped carrot and sliced celery
1 large can (1 lb. 12 oz.) pear-shaped tomatoes
2 cans (14 oz. each) regular strength beef broth
1 teaspoon sugar
½ teaspoon each pepper and ground nutmeg
½ cup salad macaroni
2 tablespoons minced parsley
    Salt
    Grated Parmesan cheese

Heat salad oil and butter in a Dutch oven over medium-high heat; add the onion and sauté until limp (about 3 minutes). Add the meat and stir over the heat until it loses its pinkness. Add the eggplant, garlic, carrots, celery, tomatoes and their liquid (break up tomatoes with a fork), beef broth, sugar, pepper, and nutmeg. Cover and simmer about 30 minutes. Add the macaroni and parsley, cover, and simmer about 10 minutes more or until macaroni is tender. Season to taste with salt.

Serve in large heated soup bowls. Pass Parmesan cheese to sprinkle over individual servings. Makes 6 to 8 servings.

Flash-in-the-Pan Recipes

Thai Egg and Beef Platter

Everyday ingredients result in a distinctive combination here: scrambled eggs smother a stir-fried dish of beef and green beans.

  1 *tablespoon salad oil or olive oil*
  1 *small onion, finely chopped*
  2 *medium-sized carrots, thinly sliced*
  1 *pound lean ground beef*
  1 *package (9 oz.) frozen cut green beans, thawed*
1½ *teaspoons salt*
  ⅛ *teaspoon pepper*
  8 *eggs*
  ¼ *cup water*
  3 *tablespoons butter or margarine*

Heat oil in a large frying pan or wok over medium-high heat; add onion and carrots and stir-fry 2 minutes; push to the sides of the pan. Add meat and stir-fry just until browned. Add green beans, 1 teaspoon of the salt, and the pepper; cover and cook over medium heat 3 minutes longer or until the beans are tender-crisp. Spoon meat mixture down the center of a large oval platter; keep warm.

Beat eggs slightly with water and the remaining ½ teaspoon salt. Melt butter in a large frying pan over medium heat and, when it foams, pour in egg mixture. Scramble eggs gently by lifting from the bottom and letting the liquid portion run underneath. When eggs are set but still creamy, spoon over the center of the meat mixture, letting meat show at the ends. Makes 4 to 6 servings.

Ground Beef Burgundy

This entrée is a good choice to serve unexpected guests; it goes together quickly with supplies from your kitchen shelf.

1 *pound lean ground beef*
1 *tablespoon all-purpose flour*
1 *cup Burgundy*
2 *tablespoons onion soup mix*
1 *can (3 or 4 oz.) sliced mushrooms*
¼ *teaspoon thyme leaves*
¼ *bay leaf*
1 *clove garlic, minced or mashed*
1 *tablespoon chopped fresh parsley*
  Hot cooked hominy, rice, or noodles

In a large frying pan over medium-high heat, cook the beef until crumbly. Add flour; stir into meat and brown slightly. Add wine, onion soup mix, mushrooms, thyme, bay leaf, and garlic. Simmer, uncovered, for about 5 minutes or until liquid is slightly reduced, stirring occasionally. Remove bay and turn into a serving dish; sprinkle with chopped parsley. Serve over hot cooked hominy, rice, or noodles. Makes 4 servings.

Quick Sloppy Joes

Pickle relish gives a sweet, spicy flavor to this version of a Sloppy Joe.

    ½ teaspoon salt
    1 pound lean ground beef
    1 medium-sized onion, chopped
    ¼ teaspoon pepper
    1 can (6 oz.) tomato paste
    ⅔ cup water
    ½ cup sweet pickle relish
    4 hamburger buns, split and toasted

Sprinkle salt in a frying pan over medium-high heat; crumble ground beef into pan, add onion and cook, stirring, until meat is brown and onions are limp (about 5 minutes). Drain any fat. Stir in the pepper, tomato paste, water, and pickle relish. Reduce heat and simmer, uncovered, 1 to 2 minutes or until heated through. Spoon meat mixture over toasted buns. Makes 4 servings.

Saturday Night Sandwich

In spite of its name, this spur-of-the-moment sandwich makes a satisfying entrée for lunch or a late supper any day.

    1 pound lean ground beef
    1 tablespoon butter or margarine
    1 medium-sized onion, chopped
    ½ green pepper, seeded and chopped
    1 can (about 1 lb.) kidney beans
    1 cup prepared barbecue sauce
      Salt and pepper to taste
    4 large soft French rolls
      Butter or margarine
    8 slices sharp Cheddar cheese

Cook ground beef in a large frying pan over medium heat in the 1 tablespoon butter. Stir until crumbly and browned. Add the onion and green pepper and cook for about 5 minutes longer until onion is soft. Discard any fat. Add kidney beans, including the liquid, and the barbecue sauce. Add salt and pepper to taste.

Simmer slowly, uncovered, while you prepare the rolls. Split rolls, spread lightly with butter, and place, cut surfaces up, on a baking sheet. Put a slice of cheese on each roll half. Put into a 400° oven until cheese melts (about 5 minutes). Remove from oven and arrange 1 or 2 roll halves on each plate. Spoon the hot meat mixture over each roll half. Serve with knife and fork. Makes 4 to 8 servings.

Jicama and Beef Sauté

Jicama (hee-cah-mah), a popular Mexican root vegetable that looks like a giant brown turnip, has crisp, white flesh that is good raw (sliced and eaten with salt) or cooked. Oriental cooks often use it as an economical substitute for water chestnuts. When sautéed for several minutes, it develops a mellow, sweet taste.

    1 large head iceberg lettuce or 2 large heads
      butter lettuce or romaine
    1 pound jicama
    1 cup regular strength beef broth
    2 tablespoons cornstarch
    1 teaspoon each sugar and grated fresh ginger
      (or minced candied ginger)
    3 tablespoons each soy sauce and dry Sherry
    ⅛ teaspoon liquid hot pepper seasoning
    2 cloves garlic, minced or mashed
    1 pound lean ground beef
    2 tablespoons salad oil
    ¾ cup chopped green onion, including part of tops
      Additional chopped green onions for garnish

Wash, drain, and chill the lettuce. Peel and cut the jicama in ⅛-inch-thick slices about ½ inch square. You should have about 3 cups. Set aside.

Gradually blend the beef broth with the cornstarch; then add the sugar, ginger, soy sauce, Sherry, hot pepper seasoning, and garlic; set this cornstarch mixture aside.

In a wide frying pan over medium-high heat, crumble the ground beef and cook, stirring, until meat is browned and juices have evaporated; takes 5 to 8 minutes. Spoon meat out of pan and set aside, discarding any fat. Add the salad oil to pan and stir in the jicama; cook, lifting and turning with a spatula just until hot.

Add cornstarch mixture and cook, stirring, until sauce boils and thickens. Blend in beef and heat (or let cool and reheat to serve); stir in the ¾ cup chopped green onion just before serving.

As an appetizer, keep the sauté mixture hot in a chafing dish (one with a hot water bath) or in a bowl on an electric warming tray. Top with additional chopped green onions and spoon bite-size portions onto sections of lettuce.

As a main dish, spoon the hot sauté mixture into large lettuce leaves on individual plates, sprinkling with additional onions. Makes 3 main dish servings or 6 to 8 appetizer servings.

Joe's Special

This favorite San Francisco dish of eggs, ground beef, and spinach dates back to the 1920s. The number of eggs used can vary to suit your taste; the more you use, the more cohesive the mixture will be.

    2 pounds lean ground beef, crumbled
    2 tablespoons olive oil or salad oil
    2 medium-sized onions, finely chopped
    2 cloves garlic, minced or mashed
    ½ pound mushrooms, sliced (optional)
    1¼ teaspoons salt
    ¼ teaspoon each ground nutmeg, pepper, and
        oregano leaves
    1 package (10 oz.) frozen chopped spinach,
        thawed and well drained, or ½ pound fresh
        spinach, washed, drained, and chopped
        (about 4 cups)
    4 to 6 eggs

Brown ground beef well in oil in a large frying pan over high heat. Add onions, garlic, and mushrooms (if used); reduce heat and continue cooking, stirring occasionally, until onion is soft. Stir in salt, nutmeg, pepper, oregano, and spinach; cook for about 5 minutes longer. Add eggs; stir mixture over low heat just until eggs begin to set. Makes 4 to 6 servings.

Quick Hamburger Hash

Soy sauce gives this dish its zesty flavor.

    3 tablespoons salad oil
    1 pound lean ground beef
    ½ medium-sized onion, chopped
        Dash pepper
    ¼ cup soy sauce
    2 cups shredded raw potato

Heat oil in a large frying pan over medium-high heat. Crumble in the ground beef, add onion, and cook until beef is well browned. Stir in pepper and soy sauce. Mound potatoes over meat, cover pan, turn heat to medium-low, and cook for 20 to 25 minutes, stirring occasionally from the bottom.

You can serve the hash at this point, but the

potatoes will not be crisp. If you prefer crisp potatoes, remove the cover after 20 minutes of cooking and continue to cook, stirring, until the potatoes brown slightly on all sides. Makes 4 servings.

Tropical Beef on Crisp Noodles

Skillet-toasted coconut and ground beef are combined with a pineapple juice sauce for a sweet-sour entrée to serve over crisp noodles.

    1 cup flaked coconut
    1 pound lean ground beef
        Salad oil
    ½ teaspoon salt
    ¼ teaspoon ground nutmeg
    1¼ cups pineapple juice
    2 teaspoons lemon juice
    2 tablespoons cornstarch
    ½ cup water
    1 can (about 6 oz.) chow mein noodles
    3 tablespoons chopped salted almonds

Stir coconut in a frying pan over medium heat until golden brown and crisp; remove and set aside. In the same frying pan, brown the ground beef, adding a small amount of oil if needed. Add salt, nutmeg, and coconut. Combine pineapple juice and lemon juice and add to beef mixture. Mix cornstarch and water until smooth. Stir into beef mixture; cook, stirring, until liquid is thickened and all ingredients are coated with sauce. Arrange fried noodles on a platter and top with coconut-beef mixture. Garnish with a sprinkling of salted almonds. Makes 4 servings.

Spanish Rice with Beef

The rice and beef simmer together in a spicy sauce for this supper entrée. Serve with a tossed green salad and crusty bread.

1½ tablespoons butter or margarine
1¼ cups uncooked rice
  1 medium-sized onion, finely chopped
  1 clove garlic, minced or mashed
  1 pound lean ground beef
  1 can (1 lb.) tomatoes
  1 can (6 oz.) mushroom sauce
  1 can (8 oz.) tomato sauce
  1 can (3 or 4 oz.) mushroom stems and pieces
 ¼ teaspoon each oregano leaves, chile powder, and pepper
  1 teaspoon salt

Heat butter in a frying pan over medium heat. Add rice and sauté along with onion and garlic until golden. Add meat and cook, stirring, until meat is browned and crumbly. Add tomatoes and their liquid, mushroom sauce, tomato sauce, mushrooms and their liquid, oregano, chile powder, pepper, and salt; mix well. Cover and simmer over low heat, stirring once or twice, for 1 hour or until rice is tender. Makes 6 servings.

Macaroni-Beef Skillet Supper

This recipe can be easily doubled; freeze the extra to be reheated for another quick dinner.

  1 cup elbow macaroni
    Boiling salted water
  2 pounds lean ground beef
  1 cup diced onion
  1 clove garlic, mashed
  2 tablespoons salad oil
  1 can (8 oz.) tomato sauce
  1 cup catsup
  2 cans (3 or 4 oz. each) mushroom stems and pieces, drained
  2 tablespoons Worcestershire
  1 teaspoon salt
 ½ teaspoon Italian seasoning (or ⅛ teaspoon each thyme, rosemary, oregano, and basil leaves)
    Dash pepper

Cook macaroni in boiling salted water following directions on package; drain and set aside. In a large frying pan over medium heat, sauté the ground beef, onion, and garlic in the salad oil until the meat is browned and onions are limp. Discard any fat. Then add tomato sauce, catsup, mushrooms, Worcestershire, salt, Italian seasoning, and pepper. Bring mixture to a boil and simmer gently, uncovered, about 5 minutes. Add the cooked macaroni and simmer, uncovered, for 5 more minutes. Makes about 6 servings.

Beef and Sausage Pepper Shells

Stuff the hot meat filling into sweet red bell peppers, then slip them under the broiler to melt the cheese topping.

  3 large red bell peppers
    Boiling salted water
  2 chorizo sausages (about 6 oz.)
  1 pound lean ground beef
 ¼ cup finely minced onion
  1 canned California green chile, seeded and chopped
 ½ teaspoon each salt and ground mace or nutmeg
 ¼ teaspoon each pepper and ground allspice
 ¼ cup finely chopped blanched almonds
 ⅓ cup chile sauce
  1 cup shredded Longhorn Cheddar cheese

Cut peppers in half lengthwise; cut out stems, seeds, and pulp. Drop into boiling water and cook, uncovered, for 4 minutes; remove; turn cut side down to drain.

Meanwhile, remove casings from chorizos; crumble into a frying pan, add ground beef and onion, and sauté over medium-high heat until meats are crumbly and brown (5 to 7 minutes). Drain off excess fat. Stir in green chile, salt, mace, pepper, allspice, almonds, chile sauce, and ¼ cup of the cheese. Cook, stirring, until cheese is melted. Spoon mixture into pepper shells; sprinkle remaining cheese over top. Place peppers in a shallow pan and broil about 6 inches from heat for 3 to 5 minutes or until cheese is bubbly and lightly browned. Makes 6 servings.

Turkish Beef

Young nasturtium leaves and freshly opened flowers garnish this beef mixture. Allow 2 to 3 leaves and flowers for each person. If you're in the habit of spraying your plants, be sure to use a spray designated for vegetable crops, and don't use it just before picking.

2 tablespoons butter or margarine
1 small onion, minced
1 clove garlic, minced or mashed
½ pound lean ground beef
1 beef bouillon cube dissolved in ¼ cup
   hot water
¼ teaspoon paprika
½ can (6 oz. size) tomato paste
½ teaspoon ground allspice
   Salt and pepper
3 tablespoons dry Sherry or 1½ tablespoons
   wine vinegar
   Turmeric Rice (recipe follows)
   Nasturtium leaves and flowers

Melt butter in a frying pan over medium heat and sauté onion and garlic until golden. Add meat and stir until crumbly and lightly browned. Discard fat. Mix bouillon mixture with paprika, tomato paste, and allspice; add to meat, stirring constantly. Add salt and pepper to taste and Sherry or vinegar; stir until liquid is nearly gone. Serve in a ring of Turmeric Rice, garnished with nasturtium leaves and flowers. Makes 2 servings.

Turmeric Rice. Prepare ½ cup long grain rice as directed on the package for steaming, adding ¼ teaspoon salt, ½ teaspoon salad oil, and ¼ teaspoon ground turmeric. When done, pat into lightly greased ring mold, cool slightly, turn out, and fill with beef.

Spicy Lamb Chile

Make this ahead and reheat at mealtime. Use canned red kidney beans to speed the preparation.

1 pound each lean ground lamb and beef
1 large onion, chopped
2 cloves garlic, minced or mashed
1 can (8 oz.) tomato sauce
1 can (6 oz.) tomato paste
1 teaspoon each celery salt and caraway seed
¼ to ½ teaspoon crushed dried red pepper
2 tablespoons chile powder
¼ teaspoon crushed bay leaf
1 teaspoon basil leaves
1 large can (1 lb. 11 oz.) red kidney beans,
   including their liquid
   Seasoned salt and pepper to taste
   Chopped onion
   Shredded Cheddar cheese

In a Dutch oven over medium-high heat, crumble the lamb and beef. Cook, stirring, until meat is browned and most of the meat juices have evaporated; discard any excess fat. Add onion and garlic and cook, stirring, until onions are limp and translucent. Stir in the tomato sauce, tomato paste, celery salt, caraway seed, crushed red pepper, chile powder, bay leaf, and basil. Add kidney beans and liquid. Bring to boiling, then reduce heat, cover, and simmer gently for about 30 minutes to blend flavors.

If you like quite thick chile, continue cooking chile, uncovered, until reduced to the thickness you like, stirring occasionally. Season to taste with salt and pepper.

When you serve the chile, pass bowls of chopped onion and shredded Cheddar cheese at the table to spoon over each serving. Makes 8 to 10 servings.

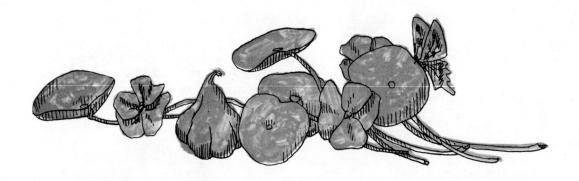

Ground Beef Curry

You can quickly stir together this ground beef dish. Pine nuts lend distinction to the curried sauce. For condiments, use sliced green onions, crisp bacon, and raisins plumped in wine.

    1 medium-sized onion, chopped
    1 tablespoon salad oil
    1 pound lean ground beef
    1 package (1¾ oz.) pine nuts
      Salt and pepper to taste
 1½ teaspoon curry powder
    ¼ teaspoon garlic salt
    1 can (8 oz.) tomato sauce
    1 cup water
    ¼ cup finely chopped parsley
      Hot cooked rice or cracked
        wheat (bulgur)
      Assorted condiments (see above)

In a large frying pan over medium-high heat, sauté onion in oil until golden. Add ground beef, pine nuts, salt and pepper to taste, curry powder, and garlic salt. Cook until meat is browned, stirring with a fork to keep it crumbly. Discard any fat. Pour in tomato sauce and water. Simmer, uncovered, for 5 minutes longer or until slightly thickened. Just before serving, stir in chopped parsley and cook just until heated through. Serve over cooked rice or cracked wheat. Pass condiments. Makes 4 servings.

Burger Rarebit

You can stir this together quickly for lunch or a late evening snack.

    1 pound lean ground beef
    ½ cup chopped onion
    1 small clove garlic, minced or mashed
    1 cup shredded sharp Cheddar cheese
    1 teaspoon prepared mustard
    5 drops liquid hot pepper seasoning
    ¼ cup catsup
    1 can (10¾ oz.) condensed Cheddar cheese soup
      Salt and pepper to taste
      Toast slices
      Paprika or chopped parsley for garnish

In a frying pan over medium-high heat crumble beef; add onion and garlic and cook, stirring until meat has lost its pinkness. Discard any fat. Reduce

heat and add cheese, mustard, hot pepper seasoning, catsup, and soup. Stir over low heat until cheese is melted and blended. Add salt and pepper to taste. Serve over toast garnished with paprika or parsley. Makes 4 to 6 servings.

Quick Chile with Coriander

Mexicans serve bowls of hot chile con carne topped with avocado slices and lots of fresh coriander leaves.

    ¾ teaspoon salt
    1 pound lean ground beef
    1 medium-sized onion, chopped
    1 can (14 oz.) pear-shaped tomatoes
    1 large can (1 lb. 11 oz.) red kidney beans
 1½ teaspoons chile powder
    1 teaspoon oregano leaves
    ½ teaspoon ground cumin seed
      Avocado slices
    ¼ cup coarsely chopped coriander leaves

Heat the salt in a 10-inch frying pan over medium-high heat; put in the ground beef and the onion; cook, stirring until browned (about 5 minutes). Discard any fat. Stir in tomatoes and their liquid, kidney beans and their liquid, chile powder, oregano, and cumin. Simmer, uncovered, stirring occasionally for about 15 minutes. Garnish each serving with several avocado slices and pass the chopped coriander. Makes about 4 servings.

Avocado Ground Beef

Avocado enriches and colors the tangy yogurt sauce.

 1½ pound lean ground beef
    1 medium-sized onion, chopped
    ½ teaspoon salt
    ¼ teaspoon each garlic salt and pepper
    1 can (10½ oz.) condensed cream of
        mushroom soup
      Water
    1 cup unflavored yogurt
    1 medium-sized avocado, cubed
    3 cups hot steamed rice

In a large frying pan over medium-high heat, lightly brown the ground beef. Add onion, salt, garlic salt, and pepper. Cook, uncovered, stirring often until onion is limp. Discard any fat. Blend in soup and cook for 5 minutes more. (Add a little water if mixture seems too thick.) Fold in yogurt and avocado; heat through but do not boil. Serve immediately with rice. Makes 4 to 6 servings.

Beef and Rice in Grape Leaves

Stuffed grape leaves, called *dolmathes* **in Greek, can be prepared with a variety of fillings. This one uses ground beef. You can find canned grape leaves in specialty food shops; or you can use cabbage leaves in place of grape leaves (let them stand in boiling water until they are quite pliable, then remove from water and trim away the thick stem).**

  1 *pound lean ground beef*
  1 *large onion, chopped*
 ½ *cup uncooked rice*
  3 *tablespoons butter or margarine*
 ½ *cup chopped parsley*
 ¼ *cup chopped mint leaves*
    Salt and pepper to taste
  1 *teaspoon dill weed*
    About 4 dozen grape leaves, canned or fresh
  1 *cup water*
  3 *eggs*
  3 *tablespoons lemon juice*

Combine ground beef, onion, rice, butter, parsley, mint, salt and pepper to taste, and dill. Wash grape leaves in hot water; drain well. Spread each leaf on a flat surface with the under side up and the stem end toward you; cut off stem. Place about 2 teaspoons of filling near the stem end, then fold the sides of the leaf over the filling and roll away from you. Continue until all the filling is used. Place the rolls in a large kettle (at least 6-quart size) on a layer of grape leaves. Add water and place a heat-proof plate on top of the rolls to prevent them from breaking apart. Cover pan and simmer for 40 minutes or until rice is cooked (break one apart to test). Drain rolls, saving the cooking liquid. Beat eggs until whites and yolks are well blended; beat in lemon juice. Bring cooking liquid to a boil; gradually add to egg mixture, beating constantly. Pour sauce over the rolls. Makes 8 to 10 servings (about 40 rolls).

Vegetable Beef Combo

This hearty, economical entrée combines diced vegetables and ground beef in a sour cream sauce.

  2 *tablespoons butter or margarine*
  2 *medium-sized onions, chopped*
1½ *pounds lean ground beef*
  1 *medium-sized potato, peeled and diced into*
    ½-inch pieces
  1 *medium-sized turnip, peeled and diced into*
    ¼-inch pieces
  3 *medium-sized carrots, in ¼-inch slices*
  2 *stalks celery, in ¼-inch slices*
 ¼ *teaspoon caraway seed*
  1 *teaspoon seasoned salt*
 ½ *teaspoon paprika*
 ⅛ *teaspoon pepper*
  1 *cup sour cream*
  1 *tablespoon all-purpose flour*
  1 *tablespoon chopped parsley*

In a large frying pan with a lid, melt butter over medium-high heat. Add onions and stir occasionally until limp. Add ground beef and break apart; cook until browned (about 5 minutes).

Then stir in potato, turnip, carrots, celery, caraway, salt, paprika, and pepper. Reduce heat to medium; then cover and cook until vegetables are just tender (15 to 20 minutes); stir frequently.

Stir together sour cream and flour; stir into pan and boil for 1 minute, stirring. Transfer mixture to serving dish and sprinkle chopped parsley over all. Makes 4 to 6 servings.

Broiled Chile-Cheese Muffins

You prepare the makings for these sandwiches on top of the range.

  1 *tablespoon butter or margarine*
 ½ *cup chopped onion*
  1 *clove garlic, minced or mashed*
 ¾ *pound lean ground beef*
 ½ *cup catsup*
  1 *tablespoon chile powder*
  1 *can (2 oz.) sliced ripe olives, drained*
  6 *English muffins, split, buttered, and toasted*
    About 6 ounces sliced jack cheese

In a frying pan, melt the butter over medium heat; add the onion and garlic and sauté until onion is limp (about 5 minutes). Add the beef and cook until brown and crumbly; drain off any fat that cooks out of meat. Stir in catsup, chile powder, and ripe olives. Spread meat mixture on 6 of the muffin halves; top with cheese. Broil 4 inches from heat until cheese melts. Top with the remaining muffin halves. Makes 6 sandwiches.

The Italian Touch

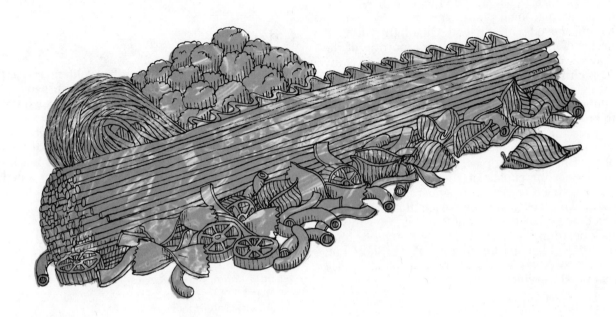

Quick Beef Pizza

Here is one way to expand a package of pizza mix into a hearty ground beef main dish pie.

    1 package (12 to 16 oz.) regular pizza mix or
        pizza mix with cheese
    1 teaspoon salt
    1½ pounds lean ground beef
    1 small onion, chopped
    ½ teaspoon oregano leaves
    1 teaspoon prepared mustard
    1 can (4 oz.) sliced mushrooms,
        drained (optional)
    1¼ cups shredded teleme or jack cheese

Prepare crust as directed on the package of pizza mix; pat out and fit into bottom and part way up the sides of a 9 by 13-inch greased baking pan. Bake, uncovered, in a 425° oven for 12 to 15 minutes or until lightly browned.

Meanwhile, heat salt in a frying pan over medium-high heat; add meat and sauté until pinkness is gone. Stir in onion and cook until limp. Discard any fat. Blend in oregano, mustard, mushrooms (if used), contents of packet of seasonings from pizza mix, cheese (if included in mix), and pizza sauce. Cook, uncovered, over medium heat for about 2 minutes to partly reduce

liquid. Pour into baked crust. Top with teleme or jack cheese. Return to the 425° oven until heated and cheese melts and browns lightly (about 10 minutes). Makes about 8 servings.

Italian-Style Pizza

Everyone loves pizza, but not everyone is up to making the dough from scratch. This quick version starts with frozen bread dough that you simply roll and stretch to fit the pans.

    1½ pounds lean ground beef
     3 cans (14 oz. each) pear-shaped tomatoes
     1 can (6 oz.) tomato paste
     1 teaspoon basil leaves
     ½ teaspoon each rosemary leaves and
         oregano leaves
     1 loaf (1 lb.) frozen bread dough
        Olive oil
     2 cups shredded mozzarella cheese
        Sliced olives, chopped onions, sliced sausage,
        or pepperoni

Crumble the ground beef into a frying pan. Cook over medium heat, stirring until meat looses pinkness. Drain all fat. Add the tomatoes and their liquid (break up tomatoes), tomato paste, basil, rosemary, and oregano. Boil rapidly, uncovered, stirring occasionally until thick and reduced to about 2½ cups.

Meanwhile, thaw the bread dough following package directions and divide dough in half. Grease two 13-inch pizza pans (or 12 by 15-inch baking sheets) with olive oil. On a lightly floured pastry cloth, roll and stretch each portion of the thawed dough into a 12-inch circle (or 9 by 14-inch rectangle); transfer to pans. Brush olive oil over surface of dough. Bake, uncovered, in a 500° oven for 4 minutes or until crust just begins to brown.

Take the two pizza bases from the oven and spread half of the beef mixture to within ½-inch of the rim of each; top each with half the cheese. Sprinkle your choice of sliced olives, chopped onions, sliced sausage, or pepperoni (or some of each) evenly over the top of each. Bake one pizza at a time, uncovered, in a 500° oven on the lowest rack position for 12 to 15 minutes longer or until crust is golden and topping is bubbly. Serve hot; cut into wedges. Makes 2 pizzas or about 4 to 6 main dish servings.

Ground Beef Pie

You press the seasoned meat mixture over the bottom and sides of a 9-inch pie pan to form the "crust" for this pizza.

1 *pound lean ground beef*
1 *egg*
2 *tablespoons each fine dry bread crumbs and finely chopped onion*
 About 1 teaspoon salt
¼ *teaspoon pepper*
1 *teaspoon Italian seasoning (or ¼ teaspoon each rosemary, basil, oregano, and thyme leaves), crushed*
2 *medium-sized tomatoes*
1 *green pepper*
1 *cup shredded jack or Cheddar cheese*
1 *teaspoon oregano leaves*

In a bowl combine the beef, egg, crumbs, onion, 1 teaspoon of the salt, pepper, and Italian seasoning; mix until well blended. Lightly press the meat mixture over the bottom and sides of a 9-inch pie pan. Peel and slice the tomatoes; seed the green pepper and cut across into ¼-inch rings. Arrange the tomato and green pepper slices on top of meat; sprinkle vegetables lightly with salt. Distribute the cheese and oregano over top.

Bake, uncovered, in a 400° oven for 25 minutes or until meat is cooked through. Use 2 spatulas to lift it out onto a serving plate. Cut into wedges to serve. Makes 4 servings.

Calzone

Calzone (kahl-*tsoh*-neh), a puffy, golden crescent packed with cheese and flavored with sausage and spicy sauce, is a sophisticated city cousin of the popular pizza.

Rolling refrigerated rolls for the dough and using canned sauce for seasoning make this calzone especially fast. Served alone as a substantial snack or combined with a green salad and soup for an easy supper, it is a table treat.

1 *can (about 10 oz.) refrigerated parkerhouse rolls*
1 *can (8 oz.) tomato sauce with onion*
1 *teaspoon each basil and oregano leaves*
2 *mild Italian pork sausages (about 6 oz.)*
 Water
 About 3 tablespoons olive oil
2¼ *cups (8 oz.) freshly shredded mozzarella cheese*
1½ *cups (5 oz.) freshly shredded Romano or Parmesan cheese*

Open rolls and let stand until warmed to room temperature. Heat tomato sauce with basil and oregano; set aside. Simmer sausages in water to cover for 20 minutes; drain, cool, remove casing, and slice thinly.

For each calzone, compress half the rolls into a flat cake and roll on a floured board to make an 11-inch diameter circle. Brush lightly with oil and spread half the tomato sauce over half the dough circle to within ½-inch of edge. Top sauce with half the sausage; sprinkle with half the mozzarella and half the Romano cheeses.

Fold plain half over filling to within ¼-inch of bottom edge. Roll bottom edge up over top edge; pinch or crimp together. Brush with oil; transfer with spatula to greased baking sheet. Bake, uncovered, in a 500° oven for 6 minutes or until golden brown. Makes 2 calzone, enough for 4 supper servings.

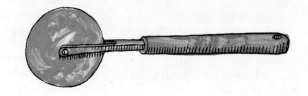

Cheese-Filled Lasagne

Big and satisfying is the nature of this meaty lasagne casserole; it waits in the refrigerator, ready to bake and serve whenever you're ready to eat.

    1 pound mild Italian pork sausage, casings
        removed and meat crumbled or chopped
1½ pounds lean ground beef
    2 stalks celery, chopped
    2 carrots, chopped
    1 large onion, chopped
    1 large can (1 lb. 12 oz.) plus 1 small can (14 oz.)
        pear-shaped tomatoes
    2 cans (6 oz. each) tomato paste
  ½ teaspoon salt
    2 teaspoons oregano leaves
  ¼ teaspoon pepper
    1 package (10 oz.) lasagne, cooked and drained
        according to package directions
        Cheese Filling (recipe follows)
    1 pound mozzarella cheese, thinly sliced

In a large saucepan or Dutch oven, combine sausage, beef, celery, carrots, and onion and cook over medium-high heat, stirring frequently until meat is just beginning to brown and vegetables are slightly soft. Add both cans of tomatoes and liquid (cutting tomatoes in chunks), tomato paste, salt, oregano, and pepper. Simmer, uncovered, for about 30 minutes or until sauce is very thick; stir frequently to prevent sticking.

Remove sauce from heat and let stand undisturbed for about 10 minutes, then spoon off and discard as much of the accumulated fat as possible. Spoon half the sauce into a shallow 3½ to 4-quart casserole, spreading it out evenly. Cover the sauce with an evenly distributed layer of half the cooked lasagne noodles. Spoon all the cheese filling onto lasagne, spreading evenly. Cover with the remaining lasagne noodles and top with the rest of the sauce. At this point you can cover and chill the casserole.

Bake, lightly covered, in a 375° oven for 30 minutes (45 minutes if chilled) or until bubbling, then uncover and quickly arrange mozzarella slices over the surface. Return casserole to the oven for 15 minutes to melt cheese. Let casserole stand about 5 minutes before cutting into rectangles. Serve with wide spatula. Makes 8 to 10 servings.

Cheese Filling. Stir together 3 cups (1½ pts.) large curd, cream-style cottage cheese (or ricotta), 2 beaten eggs, ½ cup shredded Parmesan cheese, and 2 tablespoons minced parsley.

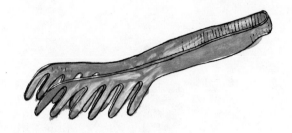

Lasagne Belmonte

Each region of Italy seems to have its own variation of the lasagne casserole. This one, using tomato and beef sauce with three flavorful cheeses, closely follows those found in the southern section.

    1 medium-sized onion, chopped
    3 tablespoons olive oil or salad oil
1½ pounds lean ground beef
    1 clove garlic, minced or mashed
    2 cans (8 oz. each) tomato sauce
    1 can (6 oz.) tomato paste
  ½ cup each dry red wine and water (or
        1 cup water)
    1 teaspoon each salt and oregano leaves
  ½ teaspoon each pepper and sugar
  12 ounces lasagne noodles
        Boiling salted water
    1 pound (2 cups) ricotta cheese or small curd
        cottage cheese
  ½ pound mozzarella cheese, thinly sliced
  ½ cup shredded Parmesan cheese

In a large frying pan over medium heat, sauté onion in oil until soft; add beef and garlic and cook, stirring, until meat is brown and crumbly. Discard any fat. Stir in tomato sauce, tomato paste, wine, and water. Add salt, oregano, pepper, and sugar. Stir until mixed. Cover pan and simmer slowly about 1½ hours.

Meanwhile, cook noodles in boiling salted water until tender as directed on package (about 15 minutes). Drain thoroughly, rinse with cold water, and drain again. Arrange about ⅓ of the noodles in the bottom of a 9 by 13-inch shallow casserole dish by crisscrossing noodles. Spread ⅓ of the tomato sauce over the noodles; top with ⅓ of the ricotta and mozzarella cheeses. Repeat this layering two more times. Top with the Parmesan cheese.

Bake. uncovered, in a 350° oven for 30 minutes or until bubbly. Makes about 6 to 8 servings.

Spicy Lasagne Variation. Substitute ½ pound mild Italian pork sausage for ½ pound of the beef. Remove the sausage casing, chop, and brown with the beef.

their liquid (break up tomatoes), tomato sauce, tomato paste, basil, oregano, thyme, parsley, salt, pepper, and rosemary. In a frying pan, sauté the mushrooms in the remaining 2 tablespoons olive oil. Add to the meat sauce and gently simmer, uncovered, until thick (about 1 hour), stirring frequently. Remove sauce from heat and let stand undisturbed for about 10 minutes, then spoon off and discard as much of the accumulated fat as possible.

Cook lasagne noodles in boiling water according to package directions; drain well. In a greased 3 by 16 by 12-inch roasting pan (or two 9 by 13-inch pans), put a layer of about half the noodles, then sprinkle with half each of the shredded mozzarella cheese, egg slices, olives, dots of ricotta cheese, then meat sauce. Repeat layers, ending with a layer of meat sauce. Top with the grated Parmesan. Bake, uncovered, in a 325° oven for 40 to 45 minutes or until heated through. Makes 12 to 18 servings.

Lasagne for a Dozen

As the name implies, this recipe is a good choice to feed a crowd—twelve very generous servings or about 18 average portions.

 1 *bunch green onions and tops, sliced*
 2 *cloves garlic, minced or mashed*
 3 *pounds lean ground beef*
 4 *tablespoons olive oil*
 2 *cans (16 oz. each) tomatoes*
 1 *can (8 oz.) tomato sauce*
 1 *can (6 oz.) tomato paste*
 1 *teaspoon each basil and oregano leaves*
 ½ *teaspoon thyme leaves*
 1 *teaspoon parsley flakes*
 1 *teaspoon salt*
 ¼ *teaspoon pepper*
 1 *teaspoon rosemary leaves*
 ¾ *pound mushrooms, sliced*
 1 *package (10 oz.) lasagne noodles*
   Boiling salted water
1½ *pounds mozzarella cheese, shredded*
 6 *hard-cooked eggs, sliced thin*
 1 *jar (3 oz.) pimiento-stuffed green olives,*
   drained and sliced
 1 *pound ricotta cheese*
1½ *cups (5 oz.) grated Parmesan cheese*

In a 5-quart kettle sauté onion, garlic, and meat over medium heat in 2 tablespoons of the olive oil until beef is crumbly. Add tomatoes and

Pasta Sauce Supreme

For a sauce that is a compromise—not as heavy as most American sauces but heavier than Italian ones—try this one.

 1 *tablespoon salad oil*
   About 6 ounces mild Italian pork sausage
   (2 medium-sized links)
 1 *medium-sized onion, chopped*
 ¼ *pound lean ground beef*
 1 *clove garlic, minced or mashed*
 1 *carrot, chopped or grated*
 1 *stalk celery, chopped*
 ¼ *pound mushrooms, sliced*
 1 *can (6 oz.) tomato paste*
 1 *can (1 lb. 12 oz.) tomatoes*
 ½ *cup dry red wine*
 1 *teaspoon basil leaves*
 ⅛ *teaspoon rubbed sage*
 ½ *cup chopped parsley*
 ½ *teaspoon salt*
 ¼ *teaspoon pepper*
   Hot cooked spaghetti, rigatoni, gnocchi, or
   other pasta
   Grated Parmesan or Romano cheese

In a 3-quart kettle, heat the oil over medium heat. Squeeze the sausage meat from the casing and break it up in the oil. Brown, stirring occasionally. Add the onion and cook until translucent, then add ground beef and brown. Stir in garlic, carrot, celery, and mushrooms, and cook for a minute or two; discard any fat. Stir in tomato paste, tomatoes and their liquid (break up tomatoes), wine, basil, sage, parsley, salt, and pepper. Turn heat to low, cover, and simmer about 2 hours or until thickened and flavors are well blended. Serve over hot cooked pasta and pass grated cheese to sprinkle on top. Makes 5 cups sauce, enough for about 6 servings.

Spaghetti-Beef Casserole with Mixed Nuts

Mixed nuts lend a crunchy richness to this baked ground beef and mushroom casserole.

      1 package (8 oz.) spaghetti
        Boiling salted water
      2 large onions, finely chopped
      2 tablespoons butter or salad oil
      2 pounds lean ground beef
   1½ teaspoons salt
      ½ teaspoon pepper
      1 can (10½ oz.) condensed tomato soup
      1 soup can water
      1 can (3 or 4 oz.) sliced or chopped
        mushrooms, drained
      ½ pound sharp Cheddar cheese, shredded
      1 teaspoon sugar
      2 tablespoons Worcestershire
      1 can (7 oz.) salted mixed nuts

Cook spaghetti in a large amount of boiling salted water according to package directions until barely tender; drain.

Using a 5-quart kettle with a tight fitting cover, sauté onions in butter over medium-high heat until limp; add beef and cook until meat is crumbly. Discard any fat. Season with salt and pepper. Stir in soup and water. Add mushrooms, ⅔ of the cheese, sugar, and Worcestershire. Then mix in the spaghetti. Turn into a greased 2½ to 3-quart casserole. Push nuts (coarsely chopped, if you wish) down into the mixture in the casserole,

sprinkling the remaining cheese on top. Bake, uncovered, in a 350° oven for 30 minutes or until heated through. Makes 8 to 10 servings.

Spicy Meat Sauce for Spaghetti

You might also serve this sauce on green (spinach-flavored) noodles. Pass Parmesan cheese at the table to sprinkle over pasta.

      1 teaspoon salt
      1 pound lean ground beef
      ½ cup each finely chopped onion, celery,
        and carrot
      2 tablespoons all-purpose flour
      1 can (6 or 8 oz.) sliced mushrooms
      2 cloves garlic, minced or mashed
      ¼ teaspoon each oregano and basil leaves
        Dash each ground cinnamon and allspice
      1 can (1 lb. 12 oz.) pear-shaped tomatoes
      1 can (8 oz.) tomato sauce
      ¾ cup dry red wine or regular strength beef broth
      ½ cup minced parsley
      ½ cup sliced pimiento-stuffed olives
        About 12 ounces spaghetti or green (spinach-
        flavored) noodles, cooked and drained
        according to package directions.
        Grated Parmesan cheese

Sprinkle salt in a large heavy frying pan over medium-high heat; add beef and sauté, stirring, about 5 minutes. Add chopped onion, celery, and carrot and continue cooking, stirring, about 5 minutes. Sprinkle flour over top; cook and stir until browned. Stir in mushrooms, including their liquid, garlic, oregano, basil, cinnamon, allspice, tomatoes and their liquid (break up tomatoes with a fork), tomato sauce, and wine or broth. Simmer, uncovered, for 30 to 45 minutes or until thickened. Stir in parsley and olives just before serving. Serve over hot, cooked spaghetti or green noodles. Pass cheese. Makes 6 to 8 servings.

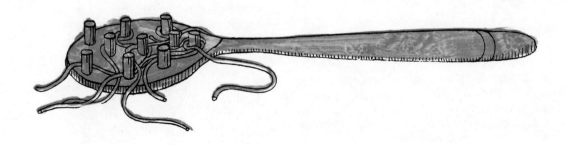

Spaghetti Beauregard

If you need a generous amount of sauce, use this recipe. If you don't use it all, freeze what's left over for another meal.

    3 tablespoons olive oil
    2 medium-sized onions, chopped
  2½ pounds lean ground beef
    3 tablespoons minced parsley
    2 teaspoons salt
    ½ teaspoon each pepper and oregano
        leaves, crushed
    ⅛ teaspoon each basil and savory leaves
    3 cans (8 oz. each) tomato sauce
    2 cans (7¾ oz. each) marinara sauce
    2 cans (6 oz. each) tomato paste
    ½ cup water
      Hot cooked spaghetti
      Grated Parmesan cheese

Heat olive oil in a 5-quart Dutch oven over medium-high heat. Add onion and cook until limp, stirring. Add ground beef, crumble, and cook until meat loses all pinkness, stirring constantly. Discard any fat. Add parsley, salt, pepper, oregano, basil, and savory, and blend. Add tomato sauce, marinara sauce, tomato paste, and water; reduce heat and simmer, uncovered, for about 45 minutes. Serve hot, or chill and then reheat when needed, spooning it over as much spaghetti as you like and topping with cheese. Makes about 2½ quarts sauce.

Meatballs in Marinara Sauce

Canned marinara sauce and Italian sausages are the seasoning shortcuts to this meatball-laden spaghetti sauce.

    ¼ pound mild Italian pork sausage,
        casings removed
    2 cans (about 1 lb. each) marinara sauce
    1 cup water
    2 pounds lean ground beef
    ⅓ cup water or regular strength beef broth
    1 teaspoon each salt and oregano leaves
    1 egg
    ¼ cup all-purpose flour
      Hot, cooked spaghetti

Crumble sausage (or chop) into a saucepan over medium heat. Brown lightly. Add the marinara sauce and 1 cup water.

Mix well the ground beef, the ⅓ cup water or broth, salt, oregano, egg, and flour.

Heat sauce to simmering. Shape beef into balls about 1 inch in diameter, dropping them into sauce as they are formed; stir gently from time to time to prevent sticking. When all the meatballs are formed, simmer in sauce for 15 minutes; skim off and discard any fat. Serve meatballs and sauce over hot, cooked spaghetti. Makes 6 to 8 servings.

Tomato Manicotti

Manicotti, a tubular filled pasta baked in a sauce, requires special effort and much time to prepare in the conventional manner. But this short-cut version saves time because you use special manicotti shells that do not require precooking (look for the package with directions on how to stuff the uncooked manicotti shells and then bake them). These dry shells, though brittle, are also easier to fill than slippery cooked ones.

    1 large can (15 oz.) tomato sauce
    ½ pound lean ground beef
    2 tablespoons chopped parsley
    2 teaspoons instant minced onion
    ¼ teaspoon each oregano and marjoram leaves
    1 cup cottage cheese
    2 cloves garlic, minced or mashed
    1 package (3¾ oz.) manicotti shells (the
        quick-cooking type)
    2 cups (8 oz.) shredded jack cheese
    ½ cup shredded Parmesan cheese

Pour ½ cup of the tomato sauce into a 2-quart shallow baking dish; set aside.

In a large bowl, combine beef, parsley, minced onion, oregano, marjoram, cottage cheese, and garlic. Mix with your hands until combined. Divide mixture equally among the 8 manicotti shells and, using your fingers, carefully stuff mixture into shells from each end. Place shells in baking dish; pour remaining sauce over shells. Cover dish with foil and bake in a 350° oven for 50 minutes.

Remove cover and sprinkle on jack and Parmesan cheeses. Return to oven, uncovered, for 10 minutes or until cheese is melted. Makes 4 servings.

Domesticating the Tortilla

Western Beef Taco

The word *taco* means a "snack," but in popular usage it has come to mean the tortilla-sandwich type snack—corn tortillas crisp-fried into a half-moon-shaped pocket and stuffed with meat filling, garnish, and spicy sauce.

    1 pound lean ground beef
    1 medium-sized onion, finely chopped
 1½ teaspoons chile powder
  ½ teaspoon each oregano leaves and paprika
  ¼ teaspoon each rosemary leaves and pepper
  ½ teaspoon salt
    3 tablespoons prepared red taco sauce
    2 teaspoons Worcestershire
      Salad oil
 10 to 12 corn tortillas
    1 small head iceberg lettuce, shredded
    2 tomatoes, cut in wedges
    1 can (4½ oz.) chopped ripe olives
  ¾ cup chopped green onion
    1 cup shredded sharp Cheddar cheese
      Bottled chile sauce or taco sauce

Brown beef in a frying pan over medium heat until crumbly; add onion and cook, stirring, until limp; discard any fat. Stir in chile powder, oregano, paprika, rosemary, pepper, salt, the 3 tablespoons taco sauce, and Worcestershire. Blend well and heat through.

Heat ¼-inch salad oil in a large frying pan over high heat. Fry tortillas one at a time about 15 seconds; fold in half and fry on each side until slightly crisp (about 30 seconds total); drain. Fill each folded taco shell with 2 to 3 tablespoons of beef filling. Keep prepared tacos warm until all are made. Pass lettuce, tomatoes, olives, green onion, cheese, and chile or taco sauce to top individual tacos. Makes 10 to 12 tacos.

Taco Salad

Typical elements of a taco—spicy meat sauce, cheese, and cold crisp lettuce—are presented here as a salad. Packaged or freshly fried tortilla chips garnish each plate.

    1 pound lean ground beef
  ¼ cup finely chopped onion
  ½ teaspoon salt
    2 teaspoons chile powder
    1 can (8 oz.) tomato sauce
    1 medium-sized head iceberg lettuce
  ½ cup shredded Cheddar cheese
    2 medium-sized tomatoes, peeled and cut
      in wedges
    1 avocado, peeled and sliced (optional)
 1½ cups tortilla chips, packaged or freshly fried

(Continued on next page)

Put beef and onion into a frying pan over medium-high heat; stir until meat is crumbly and has lost its pinkness and the onion is tender (about 7 minutes). Discard any fat. Stir in salt, chile powder, and tomato sauce; keep hot.

Shred lettuce and arrange on individual salad plates. Top each with hot meat mixture and sprinkle evenly with cheese. Garnish each salad with tomato wedges and avocado slices, if used. Place tortilla chips around edges of salads and serve immediately. Makes 4 servings.

Beef and Cheese Taco Casserole

Instead of crisp-fried tortillas, this taco casserole uses soft tortillas you spread with a little cream cheese before filling with meat.

      1 tablespoon salad oil
      2 pounds lean ground beef
      1 medium-sized onion, chopped
      2 teaspoons instant coffee powder
      1 teaspoon salt
      3 teaspoons chile powder
    ¼ teaspoon pepper
      2 cans (8 oz. each) tomato sauce
      1 package (3 oz.) cream cheese, at
          room temperature
    12 corn tortillas
    ½ cup water
      2 cups coarsely shredded longhorn
          Cheddar cheese

Heat the oil in a large frying pan over medium heat; cook ground beef, stirring, until browned; add onion and sauté about 3 minutes. Pour off excess fat. Stir in coffee powder, salt, chile powder, pepper, and 1 can of the tomato sauce. Heat to simmering.

Spread the cream cheese evenly over each of the tortillas. Place about ¼ cup of the meat mixture over cheese on one half of each tortilla; fold and arrange, with folded edge up, in a 9 by 13-inch baking dish. Pour remaining meat mixture in spaces around tortillas. Pour the remaining can of tomato sauce and then the water evenly over the top. Sprinkle with shredded cheese. Cover pan with foil and bake in a 375° oven for about 25 minutes or until heated through. Makes 6 servings.

Beef Taco-Style Casserole

Corn chips can replace tortillas in this spicy beef and bean casserole. The hot mixture is topped with chilled lettuce and sour cream just before serving.

      1 large onion, finely chopped
      1 tablespoon butter or margarine
      2 pounds lean ground beef
      1 teaspoon salt
      2 cloves garlic, minced or mashed
      2 cans (8 oz. each) tomato sauce
      2 tablespoons red or white wine vinegar
      2 tablespoons chile powder (optional)
      1 can (1 lb.) kidney beans, drained
          Crisp-Fried Corn Tortilla Chips (directions
          follow) or 1 package (about 10 oz.) corn chips
    ½ pound sharp Cheddar cheese, shredded
      2 cups shredded iceberg lettuce
      2 green onions, finely chopped
    ½ cup sour cream
      8 pitted ripe olives

In a large frying pan over medium heat, sauté onion in butter until golden. Add ground beef and cook until browned and crumbly. Discard any fat. Add salt, garlic, tomato sauce, vinegar, and chile powder, if desired. Cover and simmer 15 minutes. Mix in kidney beans.

Lightly butter a baking dish (about 10 inches square) and cover bottom with a third of the chips. Sprinkle with a third of the cheese and spoon over half the meat sauce. Add another third of the chips and cheese and remaining meat sauce. Top with the remaining chips and sprinkle with remaining cheese. (This much can be done ahead; cover and refrigerate.) Bake, uncovered, in a 375° oven for about 20 minutes (30 minutes, if refrigerated) or until bubbly.

Mix lettuce with onions and pile in the center of the hot casserole. Garnish with the sour cream and olives. Makes 8 servings.

Crisp-Fried Corn Tortilla Chips. Cut 8 corn tortillas in pie-shaped wedges (6ths or 8ths). Heat about 1 inch of salad oil in a frying pan over medium-high heat. (Temperature of oil should be 350° to 375° while cooking the chips.) Fry just a few at a time, turning occasionally until crisp and lightly browned (about 1 minute or less). Drain well; sprinkle lightly with salt. If made ahead, cool and store airtight.

Western Beef Enchiladas

In Mexico, enchiladas are served immediately after they are assembled. But the American way, geared to convenience, is to pour more sauce over the dish and bake just long enough to heat all the ingredients thoroughly. This means the enchiladas can be assembled well ahead and reheated at the last minute.

    2 cans (10 oz. each) Mexican red chile sauce or
        enchilada sauce, heated
      Ground Beef Filling (recipe follows)
      Salad oil
   12 corn tortillas
   ½ cup chopped onion
    2 or 3 cups shredded sharp Cheddar cheese
   1½ cups sour cream

Use ⅓ cup of the chile sauce and prepare Ground Beef Filling. Heat ¼-inch salad oil in a large frying pan over medium-high heat. Fry each tortilla just a few seconds until it begins to blister and becomes limp. Do not fry until firm or crisp. As soon as you take the tortilla out of the hot fat, dip it into the heated chile sauce. Lay the sauce-dipped tortilla out on a plate or pan. Spoon about 4 tablespoons of the Ground Beef Filling down the center of each tortilla and sprinkle with about 2 teaspoons onion. Roll tortilla around filling and place flap side down, in an ungreased shallow baking pan (about 9 by 13 inches). Place filled enchiladas side by side.

Pour the remaining red chile sauce over the enchiladas to moisten entire surface. Sprinkle evenly with enough shredded cheese to cover completely. Bake, uncovered, in a 350° oven for 15 to 20 minutes or just until heated through. Serve with chilled sour cream as a topping. Makes 12 enchiladas (about 6 servings).

Ground Beef Filling. In a frying pan over medium-high heat, crumble and brown 1 pound lean ground beef, adding 1 or 2 tablespoons salad oil if needed. Add 1 medium-sized onion, chopped, and cook until soft. Discard any fat. Moisten with the reserved ⅓ cup canned red chile or enchilada sauce. Slowly simmer, uncovered, for 10 minutes, stirring occasionally.

Beef and Bean Enchiladas

Here is a good casserole for a buffet meal. Let each person help himself to the sour cream and chile salsa toppings. You can assemble the casserole, refrigerate several hours.

   1½ pounds lean ground beef, crumbled
    1 medium-sized onion, chopped
    1 can (1 lb.) refried beans
    1 teaspoon salt
   ⅛ teaspoon garlic powder
   ⅓ cup prepared red taco sauce
    1 cup quartered pitted ripe olives
    2 cans (10 oz. each) enchilada sauce
      Salad oil
   12 corn tortillas
    3 cups shredded Cheddar cheese (about 10 oz.)
      Sliced pitted ripe olives for garnish
      Sour cream
      Canned green chile salsa (sauce)

In a frying pan over medium-high heat, sauté ground beef and onion until meat is browned and onion is soft. Discard any fat. Stir in beans, salt, garlic powder, taco sauce, and the 1 cup olives; heat until bubbly.

Heat enchilada sauce; pour about half into an ungreased, shallow 3-quart baking dish. Pour oil to a depth of about ¼ inch in a small frying pan; heat. Dip tortillas, one at a time, in hot oil to soften; drain quickly. Place about ⅓ cup of the ground beef filling on each tortilla and roll to enclose filling. Place seam sides down in sauce in baking dish. Pour remaining enchilada sauce evenly over tortillas; cover with cheese. Bake, uncovered, in a 350° oven for about 15 minutes or until heated through. (Or cover and refrigerate for up to 1 day; if taken directly from refrigerator, increase baking time to 45 minutes.) Garnish with olive slices. Spoon sour cream and chile salsa over each serving to taste. Makes 6 servings.

Hamburger Tostada

This recipe, geared for 1 serving, can easily be multiplied to suit a family or a crowd.

   1 *corn tortilla*
    Salad oil
   2 *or 3 tablespoons canned refried beans*
   3 *tablespoons shredded mild Cheddar cheese*
  ¼ *to ⅓ pound lean ground beef*
    Salt to taste
  ½ *cup shredded lettuce*
    Guacamole or frozen avocado dip, thawed
    Sour cream
    Prepared red taco sauce

In a small frying pan, fry the tortilla in about ¼ inch oil over medium-high heat until crisp, turning frequently; drain. (This can be done several hours ahead.)

About serving time, spread the tortilla with refried beans and Cheddar cheese; set aside. Shape beef into a patty about the size of the tortilla. Broil meat about 4 inches from heat 4 to 5 minutes on each side for medium-rare or until done to your liking. Sprinkle with salt to taste. Keep warm while you broil the tortilla about 3 inches from heat until cheese bubbles (about 1 minute). Top tortilla with the shredded lettuce, hot meat patty, and a large spoonful each of guacamole and sour cream. Pass taco sauce. Makes 1 serving.

Western Beef Tostada

A whole crisp-fried tortilla makes the bottom layer of this Mexican style open-faced sandwich. The ingredients traditionally offer contrasts of soft and crisp, hot and cold, savory or sharp and mild.

    Salad oil
  4 *corn tortillas*
  ¾ *to 1 cup canned refried beans, heated*
  ½ *cup shredded jack cheese*
    Ground Beef Filling (recipe follows)
  1 *to 2 cups shredded iceberg lettuce*
    Avocado slices
    Prepared red taco sauce

Heat about ¼-inch salad oil in a small frying pan over high heat. Fry tortillas, one at a time, about 30 seconds on each side or until crisp and lightly browned; drain.

Spread about 3 to 4 tablespoons hot refried beans over each tortilla. Sprinkle each with about 2 tablespoons cheese and add about ¼ of the Ground Beef Filling. Top with about ¼ to ½ cup shredded lettuce and garnish with avocado slices. Serve with taco sauce to spoon over. Makes 4 servings.

Ground Beef Filling. In a frying pan over medium-high heat, crumble and brown ½ pound lean ground beef, adding 1 or 2 tablespoons salad oil if needed. Add 1 small onion, chopped, and cook until soft. Discard any fat. Moisten with about ¼ cup catsup, canned red chile sauce, or enchilada sauce. Simmer, uncovered, for 5 to 10 minutes, stirring occasionally.

Chorizo Enchiladas

You make your own highly seasoned ground meat mixture to fill these enchiladas.

    Chorizo Mixture (recipe follows)
  1 *large can (1 lb. 3 oz.) enchilada sauce*
 1½ *cups each shredded jack and longhorn*
    Cheddar cheese
    Salad oil
 12 *corn tortillas*
  1 *cup sour cream*
    Pitted ripe olives for garnish
  1 *can (about 8 oz.) frozen avocado dip, thawed*

Cook chorizo mixture in a wide frying pan over medium-high heat, stirring to break meat apart and lightly brown. Add all but ¾ cup of the enchilada sauce and boil rapidly, uncovered, until liquid is gone; set aside to cool slightly. Stir in ½ cup each jack and Cheddar cheese.

In a small frying pan, heat about ¼ inch salad oil over medium heat. Fry tortillas, one at a time, just until soft; turn once. Drain briefly and dip in remaining enchilada sauce to coat all sides.

In a 9-inch square pan, overlap two tortillas to extend across one side of pan, allowing part of tortillas to extend over the rim. Spoon ⅙ of the meat mixture down center of tortillas and fold over the filling. Repeat this technique to fill remaining tortillas, placing them side by side overlapping on unfilled edges of each layer, until the pan is completely filled. Sprinkle top with remaining cheese. (This much can be done ahead; cover and chill casserole as long as overnight.) Bake unchilled casserole, uncovered, in a 350° oven until heated through (about 30 minutes); bake chilled casserole about 50 minutes, covering for the first 20 minutes. Spoon on sour cream decoratively, top with olives, and serve with avocado dip. Makes 6 to 8 servings.

Chorizo Mixture. Mix together with your hands in a large bowl 1 large, finely chopped onion; 1 pound lean ground beef; ½ pound ground pork butt; 2 teaspoons *each* chile powder and oregano leaves; ½ teaspoon ground cumin seed; ¼ teaspoon ground cinnamon; 1 teaspoon salt; ½ teaspoon liquid hot pepper seasoning (optional); and 5 tablespoons vinegar.

Making Your Own Corn Tortillas with a Tortilla Press

If you live in an area where ready-made tortillas are not sold, you can easily make your own corn tortillas from dehydrated masa flour and water, and use a hand-operated press to shape the dough into uniformly thin rounds.

A large part of the dehydrated masa flour sold in the United States is made by The Quaker Oats Company. The registered trademark of their product is Masa Harina, further identified on packages by the generic term "instant masa."

Corn Tortillas

    2 *cups dehydrated masa flour*
      (corn tortilla flour)
    1⅓ *cups warm water*

Mix masa flour with warm water until dough holds together well. Using your hands, shape dough into a smooth ball. Divide dough into 12 equal-sized pieces, then roll each into a ball.

Place a square of waxed paper on bottom half of tortilla press; place 1 ball of dough on the paper slightly off center toward the edge farthest from the handle. Flatten it slightly with the palm of your hand. Cover with a second square of waxed paper. Lower top half of the press (being careful not to wrinkle the paper), and press down firmly on lever until the tortilla measures about 6 inches in diameter. Repeat procedure, stacking the paper-covered dough rounds until all are shaped.

To cook, carefully peel off the top piece of paper from the shaped dough. Invert the tortilla, paper side up, onto a preheated, ungreased, medium-hot griddle or into a heavy frying pan over medium-high heat. As the tortilla becomes warm, you will be able to peel off the remaining paper. Bake, turning frequently, until the tortilla looks dry and is lightly flecked with brown specks (it should still be soft), 1½ to 2 minutes.

Serve tortillas immediately while still warm, or cool and wrap airtight, ready to use as directed in the accompanying recipes. Store in refrigerator for several days; freeze for longer storage (thaw before using).

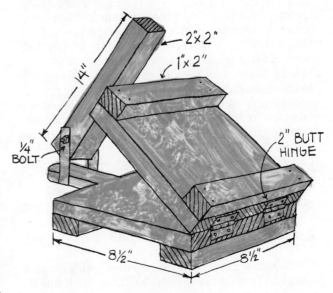

Homemade Tortilla Press

To make a wooden tortilla press, use any ¾ to 1-inch-thick wood on hand, choosing unwarped boards that will fit together evenly. Cut the paddle-shaped bottom from an 8½ by 12½-inch piece, leaving a handle on one end where you attach the 2 by 2 pressure arm. Glue and nail four 1 by 2 crosspieces to the top and bottom boards to help prevent warping when the press is washed. Attach hinges securely with long screws.

Last, locate the arm's ¼-inch bolt at a height where the arm can lever down (not completely horizontally) over the top of the press. (See illustration.)

Western Sombreros

Much like the tostada in flavor, these "sombreros" are much easier to serve and eat. You can prepare the sauce ahead and reheat it just before serving.

½ cup sliced celery
¼ cup each chopped onion and green pepper
2 tablespoons butter or margarine
1 pound lean ground beef
½ teaspoon salt
1 teaspoon chile powder
 Dash liquid hot pepper seasoning
1 can (1 lb.) tomatoes
1 can (8 oz.) tomato sauce
1 package (10 oz.) tortilla chips or corn chips
 About 1 cup shredded Cheddar cheese
 About 2 cups shredded iceberg lettuce

In a large frying pan over medium heat, sauté the celery, onion, and green pepper in the butter about 5 minutes until vegetables are limp. Add the ground beef and cook, breaking up with a fork until it loses pinkness. Discard any fat. Add salt, chile powder, and the hot pepper seasoning. Stir in tomatoes (break up with a fork) and their liquid, and tomato sauce. Simmer, uncovered, about 45 minutes to 1 hour or until sauce has thickened, stirring occasionally. To serve, spoon meat sauce evenly over tortilla chips on 4 to 6 plates, sprinkle generously with cheese, and top with shredded lettuce. Makes 4 to 6 servings.

Enchilada Casserole

For a casserole that goes together quickly, you simply layer sauce-coated tortillas with meat, chopped spinach, and cheese.

1½ pounds lean ground beef
1 small onion
1 package (1¼ oz.) taco seasoning mix
1 cup water
½ cup prepared red taco sauce
10 corn tortillas
2 packages (10 or 12 oz. each) frozen chopped
  spinach, thawed
3 cups shredded jack cheese
½ pound cooked ham, diced
1 cup sour cream

Combine beef and onion in a frying pan and brown over high heat, stirring meat to crumble. Stir in taco seasoning mix and water; cover and simmer 10 minutes.

Meanwhile, pour half the taco sauce into a 2½ to 3-quart baking dish or casserole. Dip five of the tortillas into the sauce to coat lightly. Then spread and overlap them in the bottom of the dish.

In a wire strainer, press out most of the water from spinach and stir half of the spinach into the beef; spoon the beef mixture over the tortillas in casserole and sprinkle with half the cheese.

Cover with remaining tortillas, overlapping, and spread the balance of the taco sauce over them. Distribute ham on top and spread with sour cream. Scatter the remaining spinach over the sour cream, then top evenly with remaining cheese.

Bake in a 375° oven for 50 minutes; cover for the first 25 minutes. To make ahead, assemble casserole, cover, and refrigerate; bake at 375° for 1 hour 10 minutes or until heated through and bubbling around edges; cover for the first 35 minutes. Makes 8 to 10 servings.

Picadilla

Spoon the spiced ground beef mixture into warm tortillas. Then pass shredded cheese, shredded lettuce, chopped green onion, and chopped tomatoes to embellish each serving.

¼ pound chorizos
1 pound lean ground beef
1 medium-sized onion, chopped
¼ teaspoon ground cinnamon
¼ cup raisins
1 can (4½ oz.) chopped ripe olives, drained
½ cup each catsup and water
 Warm Corn Tortillas (directions follow)
 Additional garnishes (see suggestions in the
  paragraph above)

Thinly slice or crumble the chorizos and combine with the ground beef in a frying pan over medium-high heat. Add the onion and cinnamon. Cook, stirring, until meat begins to brown. Discard any fat. Add raisins, olives, catsup, and water.

Simmer, uncovered, stirring occasionally until most of the liquid is evaporated. Serve hot or cover and chill; then reheat before serving in warmed tortillas. Garnish as desired. Makes enough for 4 to 6 servings.

Warm Corn Tortillas. Place a frying pan over medium heat. Dip your hands in water, then rub over the surface of a corn tortilla. Drop tortilla into hot ungreased pan and flip over every few seconds until it is soft, warm, and surface puffs slightly. Transfer at once to a tightly covered container or an envelope made of foil, keeping in a warm place while you heat each additional tortilla; stack together.

Chile Tostadas

Warm, soft tortillas form the base of these tostadas you broil briefly before serving. Offer accompaniments in separate bowls at the table.

6 corn tortillas
1 pound lean ground beef
½ cup chopped onion
3 to 5 tablespoons chopped canned California
    green chiles (seeds and pith removed)
½ teaspoon salt
1 can (15 oz.) chile con carne with beans
1 cup shredded jack cheese
½ medium-sized head iceberg lettuce, shredded
1 large avocado, peeled and diced
3 medium-sized tomatoes, peeled and cut
    in wedges
  Sour cream
  Prepared red taco sauce (optional)

Stack tortillas and wrap tightly in foil; place in a 350° oven for about 15 minutes to heat and soften. Meanwhile, crumble beef into a wide frying pan over medium-high heat; add onion and cook, stirring, until beef is browned and onions are limp; spoon off and discard excess fat. Stir in chiles, salt, and chile con carne. Cook, stirring, until blended and hot.

Remove tortillas from oven and arrange in a single layer on a baking sheet or oven-proof serving platter. Spoon equal portions of meat mixture onto tortillas. Divide cheese into 6 equal portions and sprinkle over meat.

Broil tostadas about 4 inches from the heat until cheese is melted (about 2 minutes). Serve immediately. Pass bowls of shredded lettuce, diced avocado, tomato wedges and sour cream to spoon over tostadas. For additional heat, drizzle with taco sauce. Makes 6 servings.

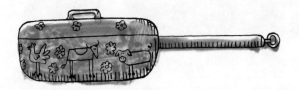

Quesadillas with Beef

Mexican cooks have many ways to stuff a tortilla. What they call a quesadilla (keh-sah-thee-ya) resembles our grilled cheese sandwich. This version also includes a ground beef mixture.

½ teaspoon salt
1 pound lean ground beef
½ cup finely chopped onion
1 clove garlic, minced
½ teaspoon oregano leaves, crumbled
1 can (8 oz.) tomato sauce
1 dozen 8-inch flour tortillas
¾ pound mild or sharp Cheddar cheese, shredded
½ cup (¼ lb.) butter or margarine

Sprinkle salt in a large frying pan and add ground beef and onion; sauté over medium-high heat, stirring until crumbly. Discard any fat. Add garlic, oregano, and tomato sauce. Let simmer, uncovered, until the liquid evaporates.

Sprinkle 1 tortilla with about ½ cup cheese and spoon over about ⅓ cup of the meat mixture. Cover with a second tortilla. Melt 2 tablespoons butter in a large frying pan over medium-high heat, lay in the filled tortillas, and cook until golden brown underneath. With a wide spatula, carefully turn and brown other side. Serve at once or place in a baking pan, uncovered, and keep warm in a 250° oven until all are fried. Continue to fill and cook the remaining tortillas in the same manner. Makes 6 servings.

Chirrasquillas

Costa Ricans garnish this dish with fried plantains. You might try green bananas if you like the idea. Slice and fry them in the same fat after all the chirrasquillas are cooked.

1 large onion, chopped
2 tablespoons butter or margarine
1 pound lean ground beef
1 teaspoon salt
  Dash pepper
  Pinch oregano leaves
¼ teaspoon chile powder
1 small clove garlic, minced or mashed
12 corn tortillas
1 cup beer or water
1 cup all-purpose flour
3 eggs
  Salad oil

In a frying pan over medium-high heat, sauté onion in butter until limp. Add beef, ½ teaspoon of the salt, pepper, oregano, chile powder, and garlic. Cook until meat browns, breaking it up with a fork. Discard any fat. Cool and divide mixture among the 12 tortillas, putting spoonfuls on the center of each. Fold over as you would turnovers and fasten with toothpicks.

Make a batter by beating together the beer or water, flour, the remaining ½ teaspoon salt, and eggs. Heat about 1½ inches of salad oil in a large frying pan to 365° to 370°. Dip folded tortillas into the batter, one at a time, and deep fat fry until crisp and lightly browned. Drain. Makes about 12 chirrasquillas.

Tortilla Pizza

The elements of a traditional pizza top these flat, crisp-fried tortillas that you can eat with your hands.

    Salad oil
  8 corn tortillas
  2 pounds lean ground beef
  1 medium-sized onion, minced
  1 clove garlic, minced or mashed
 ¼ pound mushrooms, chopped
  1 can (4½ oz.) chopped ripe olives, drained
  1 can (6 oz.) tomato paste
 ½ pound Cheddar or mozzarella cheese, shredded
    Grated Parmesan or Romano cheese (optional)

In a large frying pan over medium-high heat, heat about ¼ inch of salad oil. Fry tortillas one at a time, turning occasionally until crisp and lightly browned (about 1 minute); drain. Cook ground beef, onion, garlic, and mushrooms in a frying pan over medium-high heat until meat is browned, stirring often. Discard any fat. Add olives and tomato paste and cook, uncovered, over low heat, stirring occasionally for about 5 minutes more. Place tortillas flat on baking sheets. Top the tortillas evenly with the meat

mixture, then sprinkle evenly with the Cheddar or mozzarella cheese. Sprinkle lightly with grated cheese. Bake, uncovered, in a 425° oven for 10 minutes or until cheese melts. Makes 8 individual tortilla pizzas, enough for about 4 servings.

Taco Beef Casserole

Taco seasoning and enchilada sauce supply the spark for this tortilla-beef combination.

  1 medium-sized onion, finely chopped
  1 tablespoon salad oil or olive oil
  2 pounds lean ground beef
  1 package (about 1¼ oz.) taco seasoning mix
  1 cup water
  1 package (9 oz.) frozen corn, thawed
  1 can (6 oz.) pitted ripe olives, drained
  6 corn tortillas
  1 can (10 oz.) enchilada sauce
  2 cups shredded sharp Cheddar cheese
  1 avocado, peeled, pitted, and sliced

In a large frying pan over medium heat, sauté onion in oil until limp; push to the sides of the pan. Add the ground beef and sauté until browned, stirring. Discard any fat. Add taco seasoning and water, cover, and simmer 10 minutes. Remove from heat and add corn. Reserve ⅓ cup of olives for topping, coarsely chop remainder, and add to meat.

Cut tortillas into quarters, dip each piece into enchilada sauce, and arrange half of them in the bottom of a greased 9 or 10-inch-round baking dish (about 2 inches deep). Cover with half the meat sauce and spoon over half the remaining enchilada sauce. Sprinkle with 1 cup of the cheese. Repeat layers, ending with cheese.

Bake, uncovered, in a 350° oven for 20 minutes or until heated through. Garnish with avocado slices and remaining olives. Serves 6 to 8.

Index